The Arnold and Caroline Rose Monograph Series
of the American Sociological Association

Continuity and Change

A study of two ethnic communities in Israel

Other books in the series

J. Milton Yinger, Kiyoshi Ikeda, Frank Laycock, and Stephen J. Cutler: *Middle Start: An Experiment in the Educational Enrichment of Young Adolescents*
James A. Geschwender: *Class, Race, and Worker Insurgency: The League of Revolutionary Black Workers*
Paul Ritterband: *Education, Employment, and Migration: Israel in Comparative Perspective*
John Low-Beer: *Protest and Participation: The New Working Class in Italy*
Orrin E. Klapp: *Opening and Closing: Strategies of Information Adaptation in Society*
Marshall B. Clinard: *Cities with Little Crime: The Case of Switzerland*

Volumes previously published by the American Sociological Association

Michael Schwartz and Sheldon Stryker: *Deviance, Selves and Others*
Robert M. Hauser: *Socioeconomic Background and Educational Performance*
Morris Rosenberg and Roberta G. Simmons: *Black and White Self-Esteem: The Urban School Child*
Chad Gordon: *Looking Ahead: Self-Conceptions: Race and Family as Determinants of Adolescent Orientation to Achievement*
Anthony M. Orum: *Black Students in Protest: A Study of the Origins of the Black Student Movement*
Ruth M. Gasson, Archilbald O. Haller, and William H. Sewell: *Attitudes and Facilitation in the Attainment of Status*
Sheila R. Klatzky: *Patterns of Contact with Relatives*
Herman Turk: *Interorganizational Activation in Urban Communities: Deductions from the Concept of System*
John DeLamater: *The Study of Political Commitment*
Alan C. Kerckhoff: *Ambition and Attainment: A Study of Four Samples of American Boys*
Scott McNall: *The Greek Peasant*
Lowell L. Hargens: *Patterns of Scientific Research: A Comparative Analysis of Research in Three Scientific Fields*
Charles Hirschman: *Ethnic Stratification in Peninsular Malaysia*

Continuity and Change

A study of two ethnic
communities in Israel

Rita James Simon
University of Illinois

Cambridge University Press

Cambridge
London   New York   Melbourne

Published by the Syndics of the Cambridge University Press
The Pitt Building, Trumpington Street, Cambridge CB2 1RP
Bentley House, 200 Euston Road, London NW1 2DB
32 East 57th Street, New York, NY 10022, USA
296 Beaconsfield Parade, Middle Park, Melbourne 3206, Australia

First published 1978

Printed in the United States of America
Typeset by Ariya Company, Brooklyn, New York
Printed and bound by the Murray Printing Company, Westford, Massachusetts

Library of Congress Cataloging in Publication Data
Simon, Rita James.
Continuity and change.
(The Arnold and Caroline Rose monograph series of the
American Sociological Association)
Includes index.
1. Social surveys — Israel.
2. Jerusalem. Meah She'arim — Social conditions
3. Jews in Jerusalem — Social conditions.
4. Palestinian Arabs — Israel — Social conditions.
5. Sex role. I. Title.
II. Series: The Arnold and Caroline Rose monograph series in sociology.
HN660.A8S55   309.1'5694   77-15090
ISBN 0 521 21938 8 hard covers
ISBN 0 521 29318 9 paperback

To Julian
and for David, Judith, and Daniel

Contents

Preface

The idea for this book was conceived during our first trip to Israel in 1968. My husband and I came to Jerusalem in January to teach at Hebrew University. Our third child was born in Jerusalem a few weeks later. At that time, the Six Day War was the most recent war. It had resulted in dramatic changes in the boundaries, demography, and mood of the country. One of the important issues that the 1967 war raised was how both the Jewish Israelis and the Israeli Arabs would relate to the Arab communities in the newly occupied territories of East Jerusalem, Hebron, Nablus, and other parts of the West Bank, and the Gaza Strip. To an outsider listening to those discussions, the position and the future of the Israeli Arabs — those Arabs who had opted to remain in Israel following partition in 1948, and who have been citizens of Israel ever since — seemed more complex and problematic than the relationship between the Arabs in the occupied territories and groups within Israeli society. The adults in the Israeli Arab community had personally experienced the transition from being members of a majority group to becoming part of a minority. In large measure, they had learned how to accommodate themselves and how to survive physically, culturally, and environmentally in a Jewish state. But what of the next generation who had not personally made the choice to remain in a Jewish state and who were growing up in a period of Arab nationalism? How did those younger Israeli Arabs define their place in Israeli society, and how did they view their future in that society?

My interest in the ultra-Orthodox Jewish community has stemmed in part from personal experience. Many of my neighbors in the area of New York City in which I spent part of my childhood looked, behaved, and dressed much like the people in Mea Shearim. The street language was the same, the articles for sale and the transactions in the shops were reminiscent of my old neighborhood. But aside from these personal interests the ultra-Orthodox community held a degree of fascination because it was a closed community; or so it seemed to an outsider. Secular Israelis, and indeed even many who defined themselves as observant or traditional Jews were put off by the ultra-Orthodox. They had no personal contacts with them. They perceived them as one might inhabitants of a hostile but nearby island, critical of their government, and supercilious toward the values and the life style of most Israelis. Many of the older people in Mea Shearim were of the first generation. They came to Israel from the shtetls of Eastern Europe. Some came via the concentration camps or the displaced persons' camps. But the adolescents and young adults shared none of the experiences of the Diaspora. They, like the young Israeli Arabs, were all sabras (native-born Israelis). But they are sabras who are being socialized in a subculture that is different from and feels superior to the mainstream. Many of the same questions I wanted to put to the young Israeli Arabs were applicable to the young people in the ultra-Orthodox Jewish community of Mea Shearim.

I began asking my questions in 1968. Hebrew University provided me with funds to hire two assistants, and a colleague at the Institute of Communications, Michael Gurevitch, worked with me on the initial questionnaire. I returned to Israel in the fall of 1970, and with the assistance of a Ford Foundation fellowship and a small grant from the Center for International Comparative Studies at the University of Illinois, I was able to mount a larger and more intensive study. In the summer of 1973, and then again during our last trip to Israel in the fall of 1974, I went back to observe and talk with the people in those communities. The first draft of the manuscript was written in Jerusalem in 1975.

The problems of gaining access to ultra-Orthodox and Arab communities and the obstacles I encountered, particularly vis-à-vis the ultra-Orthodox, are described in some detail in Chapter 2. Perhaps only after reading that account will a reader be able to appreciate the extent of my debt of gratitude to my field staff. Without the tenaciousness, loyalty, and determination of Victor Tresczan, Hermona Hayutman, Yael Roten, Yeheskel Kuyama, and Joseph Kossman the survey in Mea Shearim would not have been carried out. For the data from the Arab communities, I relied most heavily on Mohammed Ibraham Atamna, whose family has lived in Baqa El Garbiya for generations. Atamna supervised a staff of Arab interviewers who worked under his direction.

Once I had written a draft of the manuscript, Elaine Jacobson,

Thelma McCormick, Julian Simon, Ida Harper Simpson, and Robin Williams provided useful criticism and suggestions that I believe considerably improved the quality of the work. I am very grateful for their help and advice.

In Jerusalem, Sylvia Farhi typed many of the early drafts, and in Urbana, Patricia Camp at the Institute of Communications Research typed the final copy. Ester Smith and Roberta Cohen helped code the questionnaire responses and analyze the data. Marcia Kirkpatrick helped find and organize many of the references. Their help is acknowledged with appreciation. To my husband and children who shared many hours with me walking around Mea Shearim and visiting families in the Arab communities, I am grateful.

One final thought. Some of the respondents in both the Arab communities and the ultra-Orthodox Jewish community explained to me on several occasions that I was dealing with extremely sensitive and delicate matters and that it was most important that I tell it "as it is" that I not exploit their situation for political or professional gain. I have tried to honor the promise I made to them.

Rita James Simon

Urbana, Illinois
January, 1978

Introduction

There are two ethnic communities in Israel that for different reasons have remained outside the mainstream of Israeli society, although the members of both have deep roots in the soil of Israel. Most of the members of these communities are not new immigrants who have settled in Israel since the establishment of the state in 1948. Rather, they are the descendants of families who have lived in the area for generations and even centuries. The two communities are Israeli Arabs, and ultra-Orthodox Jews who trace their most recent spiritual and cultural heritage to the shtetls (Jewish villages) and cities of seventeenth-, eighteenth-, and nineteenth-century Eastern Europe.[1]

This monograph presents the results of two surveys conducted among members of each of these communities to find out whether the parents in these communities have succeeded in transmitting to their adolescent children the dominant values and themes of their cultures and life styles. We explore the extent to which the adolescents have internalized their parents' values and aspirations and the extent to which they have moved toward greater contact with the mainstream of Israeli society. Each community is treated separately, but the same questions are asked of both. The key question is: What is the likelihood for intergenerational change and for more extensive contacts with the larger society on the part of the younger Israeli-born generation?

Of the two ethnic collectivities, the Arab one is the larger. Israeli Arabs represent approximately 13 percent of the total Israeli population. They live mainly in small towns and villages in the northern part of Israel, in the Galilee. The ultra-Orthodox Jews, on the other hand, number in the thousands; they live primarily in Jerusalem, in B'nai Brak, a suburb of Tel Aviv, and on a few Orthodox kibbutzim (collectives) and moshavim (cooperative settlements).

This monograph does not provide a detailed ethnographic account of the complexities of day-to-day living in these communities. Neither does it attempt a comprehensive analysis of the status of these commu-

1

nities and of their ties to the rest of Israeli society. It provides data and insights on specific characteristics and strains within these communities as perceived by respondents who represent two generations, and it offers some prognosis about the future of those communities vis-à-vis the mainstream of Israeli life and politics.

One of the most distinctive characteristics of Israeli society and a source of considerable pride to the state is the enormous success that it has had in integrating and assimilating immigrants with widely varied cultural and social backgrounds. Jews from the ghettos of Casablanca, Bagdad, and Tunis, from the Atlas mountains of Morocco, and from the villages of Yemen, and Jews from Vienna, Budapest, and Paris, from Bombay, and Johannesburg, from Buenos Aires, and Los Angeles have in one generation been transformed into Israelis who consider Tel Aviv, Beersheva, Haifa, or some kibbutz or moshav their home. They and their children dress differently, speak differently, work at different kinds of jobs, eat different kinds of food, and in general pursue a life style that is significantly different than that pursued by families of prior generations.

On the whole, the two populations that are the focus of this study did not participate in this massive resocialization program. The reasons for nonparticipation are different. The relative isolation and insulation of the ultra-Orthodox Jews from the rest of Israeli society is largely voluntary. Members of this community, although they are fully aware of their small numbers, have a deep and powerful belief in the superiority of their culture, religious beliefs, family structure, and indeed their entire way of life. At best, they look upon other Jews, especially Israelis, with pain and sorrow, at worst with scorn and disgust. They have a deep and seemingly unshakable belief in the timelessness of their culture and its values, and a realistic awareness of the precautions that must be taken to prevent assimilation into the larger culture by their younger members.

The Arab community has also remained outside the mainstream of Israeli society; but in its case the reasons are a combination of desire and lack of choice. The desire is most likely to be manifest among older members of the community who wish to maintain their cultural and religious identity. They wish, for example, to retain a distinctive language, style of dress, set of marital arrangements, and work and leisure patterns. In addition, however, Jewish Israelis have imposed barriers at the entryways of some of the more important institutions of the society, most notably the armed forces and various occupations, that make assimilation or integration extremely difficult.

As one looks ahead and considers the sources of potential discord within Israeli society, the role that these two communities are likely to play vis-à-vis the larger society takes on crucial importance. It is not daydreaming or wishful thinking to expect that Israel's relations with its Arab neighbors will one day improve, and that the Middle East will be a region of nations showing mutual respect for one another's sovereignty. It is also not wishful thinking to believe that "that day" may occur in the next generation. The cease-fire agreement between Israel and Egypt that has been in effect since the end of the Yom Kippur War (1973) and the more recently permitted exchange of visits among Druze families on the Syrian and Israeli sides of the Golan Heights may represent the beginning of a change in the relationship Israel will have with its neighboring Arab states. But what is less likely is that Israel's internal communal conflicts can or will be resolved in that same period of time. As one considers the most likely sources of internal tension and strain, differences that revolve around the religious—secular axis and the Jewish—non-Jewish axis rank high.[2]

Although the ultra-Orthodox Jewish community is small in number, its image has great importance to many Jews all over the world who live more or less secular lives. In commenting on police treatment of members of this community after the police had been called in to protect tourists who were being attacked by some of the more zealous members, the then prime minister, Ben Gurion, observed: "It is always more difficult when acts are prompted by a deep, religious belief . . . they represent a world most of us come from — they look like our grandfathers. How can you slap your grandfather into jail, even if he throws stones at you? . . . " (Leslie, 1971:146).

The term "they look like our grandfathers" is important. In their daily lives most Israelis do not participate in that regimen of prayer, dietary observances, dress, and study that regulates almost every hour and mood of an observant Jew's life. The Israeli lives a modern, secular life in which he has self-consciously discarded the sacred duties that preoccupy the ultra-Orthodox Jew. But at least half of the Jewish population in Israel have had Jewish grandfathers or great-grandfathers who have adhered to this pattern and have memories of these people that occupy special places in their consciousness. To even the most secular Israeli these memories of individual relatives are integrally tied to their memories of a whole people and a cultural past. That social or cultural memory is of Judaism and the Jewish people and their struggle for survival in what has many times been a hostile, dangerous Gentile world. Some of these grandfathers did manage to survive, and their survival is indivisibly bound to the survival of the entire people. These same secular Israelis may view that history with ambivalence, and they may ask of these relatives: Why did you live as you did in your ghettos, always fearful of the next pogrom or invasion; why did you not do as we did when we came and settled in Palestine in the 1910s and 1920s? But they are grateful, nevertheless; and they are respectful of the facts of survival. They credit that survival, perhaps grudgingly, to their grandfathers' faith, to their religious beliefs, and to the tenacity with which they held to the belief about their superiority.

Thus the secular Israeli today, when he confronts these transmitters of the faith of a culture, is often both angered and disgusted at the seeming inability of these people to make the necessary adjustments to their new environment, at their inability or unwillingness to recognize that life in Israel, a free and independent Jewish state, is qualitatively different from earlier Jewish experience since the destruction of the Second Temple. But hidden behind the disgust and the anger is the feeling that these people, after all, are "special"; they deserve to be treated in a special way, and one must "put up" with some of their demands. How many demands often becomes the crucial issue in parliamentary debates or encounters with the police.

Some measure of the success of this tiny, ultra-Orthodox community is manifested by the fact that there is no civil marriage or divorce in Israel; only the Orthodox Rabbinate is officially recognized; there is no public transportation in most of Israel on the Sabbath; and dietary laws are observed at all official functions. The ultra-Orthodox community has not been alone in insisting upon these controls. The Mizrachi Party, which is the largest of the religious parties, and indeed some Israelis who do not ordinarily vote for any of the religious parties, have also supported and argued for these measures.

For the sake of unity, during this period when external danger looms very large, most Israelis have argued against doing anything that would shake the structure and cohesion of Israeli society. Movements that would push for changes in the Sabbath observances, in the marriage and divorce laws, and in the monopoly over all religious functions by Orthodox Jewry, to name some of their most unpopular characteristics, might seriously disturb the balance at a time when severe internal conflict could be disastrous. The time for discussing basic internal changes and for insisting on these changes must follow a peaceful resolution of Israel's external problems. This argument has been persuasive for almost thirty years; it is likely to continue to be so. The ultra-Orthodox Jewish community is likely to maintain its influence on the less extreme religious groups or political parties, for example, on the Agudat, which in turn influences the Workers' Agudat, which in turn influences the Mizrachi to be certain that there is no weakening within the ranks and no internal pressures for change.

In sum, then, when one attempts to anticipate the future in Israel as far ahead as the next generation, the likelihood of internal conflict resulting in basic changes appears to be very much dependent on external affairs. Should peace come to the Middle East, it is likely to be followed by a significant increase in the amount of internal conflict and dissension between the ultra-Orthodox religious community and the rest of Israeli society. Based on the information collected in our survey, we have little doubt that the ultra-Orthodox religious community will be a formidable opponent.

The relationship of the Arab community to the rest of Israeli society and how changes in that relationship might affect the level of tension within the society involve a different set of assumptions and problems. In numbers the Israeli Arabs are a much larger and more visible community than are the ultra-Orthodox Jews. Most Israelis do not feel the same ambivalence toward them that they do toward the ultra-Orthodox Jews. The fact that Israelis did not have "Arab grandfathers" is certainly one aspect of the problem. Another, and most important of course, is the recent history of Arab-Jewish relations. In fact, whatever loyalties and sentiments Arabs living in Israel may have toward the Arab nations and toward the state of Israel, at best most Jewish Israelis are skeptical of the loyalty of Israeli Arabs to Israel. They believe that in a major conflict, if fighting were to occur within the pre-1967 boundaries, Israeli Arabs would support the Syrians, Egyptains, and Jordanians, against Israel. The fighting in June 1967 did not last long enough, and that in October 1973 did not occur on pre-67 Israeli soil or on inhabited areas; hence these expectations have not been properly tested. On the whole, over the past twenty-eight years, Israeli Arabs have engaged in relatively few overt acts of disloyalty — nor have they given much in the way of material or moral support to the Arab guerillas who succeeded in gaining entry into Israeli territory. Nevertheless, Israelis' opinions about their own Arab community are very much tied to their beliefs about the prospects for peace with the neighboring Arab states. As those beliefs become pessimistic, their ambivalence toward the Israeli Arab community increases.

Formally, on most issues, the Arab community enjoys first-class citizenship. The most significant exceptions are exemption from the army (except on a special volunteer basis), exclusion from certain occupations in "sensitive" industries, and limitations on some types of travel. The latter restrictions have been significantly reduced since 1966. Today they are almost nonexistent. Informally, however, there is widespread segregation and isolation of Jews and Arabs, and education at the elementary school level is almost completely segregated. At the high school level this is less often the case but separate schools are still the more typical pattern. Geographical segregation is also the mode: Most Arabs live in villages or towns inhabited completely by Arabs. Those who live in urban settings live mainly in Arab neighborhoods. Intermarriage is almost nonexistent.

If Israelis were to give candid responses to the question, "What in your opinion would be the optimal solution to the Israeli Arab problem?" many would say that they favor some type of equitable solution that would result in Israeli Arabs emigrating from Israel and settling elsewhere. But just as candidly they would also say that such a solution is politically impractical. A more realistic projection is that an Arab community will remain in Israel, will grow considerably over the next couple of decades, and will make greater demands on the state for more representation in the economic, political, and social spheres. If this projection is realistic, the crucial question is: How will Israel respond? And how Israel responds will significantly affect the stability and viability of the society.

The purpose of this volume is to report the findings of surveys conducted among members of both the ultra-Orthodox Jews and the urban Israeli Arab populations. The respondents were selected to represent two time perspectives: (1) the past-present perspective as represented by the parents and (2) the present-future perspective as represented by the adolescents. The major focus of the surveys was to assess the manner in which the older and younger members perceive the future of their communities both in terms of the communities' internal characteristics and their relations vis-à-vis the larger society.

In the ultra-Orthodox Jewish population, we interviewed 100 fathers and unmarried sons between the ages of sixteen and twenty-one; and 50 mothers and unmarried daughters between the ages of fifteen and twenty. All of the respondents live in the Mea Shearim section of Jerusalem. Among the Arab population, we sampled only within urban centers and only those urban areas in which there are both Arab and Jewish communities. There are five such cities in Israel: Acco, Haifa, Jaffa, Lod, and Ramle; and we sampled respondents in each of them.[3] In sum, 125 Arab fathers and sons (with the same age characteristics as the Jewish sample) and 50 Arab mothers and daughters were included.

In both the Arab and Jewish samples the parents either grew up in Israel when the country was still a British mandate, or had emigrated to Israel after spending their formative years in a shtetl or large city in Eastern Europe, or in an Arab country. But all of the children in the two samples were born and reared in an independent Jewish state.

The book is divided into two major sections. The first part provides a background and description of the two ethnic communities and compares them with communities in other parts of the world that have similar characteristics. The second part reports the result of the survey among the two communities. Chapters 1, 2, and 3 make up Part One; Chapters 4 to 10 constitute Part Two. Chapter 1 examines the ties that Israeli Arabs and the ultra-Orthodox Jewish communities have with the larger society, including their formal status as well as their informal contacts and associations. Chapter 2 describes the social and demographic characteristics of the two populations. It also reports the research plan and the obstacles encountered in collecting the data. Chapter 3 provides information about three institutions (education, politics, and mass media) that help to sustain and insulate the two communities from the larger society but that also provide bridges for the Israeli Arabs to establish contacts with the mainstream of Israeli society.

Chapters 4 and 5 provide profiles of the two communities based on the surveys. The profiles focus on the status that the parents and adolescents occupy and on the roles that each is expected to play within the two communities. Chapter 4 describes the Mea Shearim community, and Chapter 5 describes the Arab communities in the urban centers of Israel.

Chapters 6 and 7 focus on the similarities and differences in attitudes, beliefs, and behaviors that are a function of sex roles within the parents' and children's generations. Chapter 6 describes sex roles in Mea Shearim, and Chapter 7 describes sex roles in the urban Arab communities.

Chapters 8 and 9 are the heart of the study. They deal with the differences and the lack of them that are attributable to generation and to sex role within the two communities. Chapter 8 describes those characteristics in Mea Shearim, and Chapter 9 describes the same types of characteristics in the Arab communities.

Chapter 10 is the summarizing and concluding chapter. In it, basic questions about the future collective identity of each of these communities and their respective ties to the larger society are considered. The chapter also speculates about the implications of alternative modes of behavior for each of the communities as well as for the society as a whole.

PART ONE

Chapters 1, 2, and 3 provide historical, theoretical, and demographic background and descriptions that should help make the results of the survey more understandable and more relevant for assessing the importance of the two ethnic communities to the future of Israeli society. The major values and leitmotiv of the two populations are described and contrasted with those of other communities that have been, or are today, in similar circumstances in other societies.

A brief description of Israeli social structure and organization is included as a prologue to a more detailed account of the place that these two communities occupy in the larger setting. Three major institutions — politics, education, and the mass media — are selected for a more detailed description because each of them performs significant functions within the ultra-Orthodox and Arab communities. Part One does not pretend to be a thorough sociological analysis of Israeli society; however, it should provide enough information about the major characteristics of the society and the manner in which it is organized so as to provide a better fit between the survey data and the rest of Israeli society.

1. The Jewish ultra-Orthodox and the urban Arab communities: theoretical and geographical comparisons

This chapter considers the ultra-Orthodox Jewish community and the urban Arab community in Israel from the perspective of their relationships to the larger society. It asks how similar or how different are the ties that each community maintains to the dominant culture compared with the ties that other minority ethnic communities maintain in other societies. By ethnic community we mean essentially what Gordon did when he wrote:

> the ethnic group . . . [is] a large subsociety, criss-crossed by social class and containing its own primary groups of families, cliques, and associations — its own network of organizations and institutions — in other words, as a highly structured community within the boundaries of which an individual may, if he wishes, carry out most of his more meaningful life activities from the cradle to the grave. (1964:234)

As stated in the introduction, and as will be reiterated several times in various parts of this book, a major reason for deciding to study these particular communities was the different stances each of them has assumed vis-à-vis the larger society. An additional reason for studying them is that each, in adopting a particular stance, will play an important role in determining the stability and cohesiveness of Israeli society.

The stance of the Israeli Arab community (throughout the book, this community refers only to Arabs in urban centers) is the one more typically taken by minority ethnic groups that have the opportunity or the choice either to draw closer or to stand back from the larger society. Like those of Italian, Greek, Jewish, and German extraction in the United States, the Israeli Arabs, especially those born in Israel, are willing and eager to partake of much that the larger society has to offer. As will become apparent in later chapters, as soon as the fighting that had broken out following the establishment of the state was over, the Arab minority chose to participate in most of the major institutions of the society. The Arab community in Israel represents a slightly larger proportion of the total population than the black community represents in the United States. When the first parliamentary elections were held in 1949, 79 percent of the Arab community registered and voted (only 7 percent less than the percentage of Jews voting). Three Arabs were elected to that first Parliament. Since then there have been seven or eight Arabs in each Parliament.

The Israeli government continued the tradition of the Turks and the British in granting a certain degree of judicial autonomy to the Arab community, primarily in matters of personal status and in administering religious institutions. The government also provides some financial support to both the Muslim and the Christian Arab religious institutions.

Education is compulsory in Israel for both Arab and Jewish children through the primary grades. Schools are segregated, so that most Jewish children attend state-supported schools in which the language of instruction is Hebrew, and most Arab children attend state-supported schools in which the language of instruction is Arabic. For Jewish children, English is the second language, and they have a choice usually between Arabic and French as a third language. For Arab children, Hebrew is the second language. The result is that most Arabs who have grown up since the state of Israel was established can speak or understand some Hebrew, but most Jews can neither speak nor understand Arabic.

The Arab language enjoys official status. It appears together with Hebrew and English on Israeli currency and postage stamps. It can be used for pleading cases and giving evidence in courts of law and for speeches in the Knesset (Israeli Parliament). All laws are published in three different editions: Hebrew, Arabic, and English. Traffic and street signs in many, but not all parts of the country, appear in Arabic as well as Hebrew. Radio and television, which are state controlled, have designated times for programming in Arabic. Since 1960, Arab laborers have been admitted to full membership in the Histadrut (General Federation of Labor). As of 1969, about 40,000 Arab laborers had joined (Samuel, 1969:108).

In each of the ways just described, the relation of the Arab community to the larger Israeli society appears not qualitatively different from that of the Greeks or the Italians in the United States. In both instances, we see minority ethnic communities that are willing to adopt and take advantage of the opportunities and services that the larger society can provide. For example, they avail themselves of educational opportunities, political representation, financial support for their mosques and churches, welfare and medical services. But they also manifest behavior that indicates their desire to retain different and separate aspects of their community. Language, choice of marriage partners, and religious beliefs and observances are important ways in which the Arab community in Israel and the Greek and Italian communities in the United States have maintained boundaries between themselves and the larger society.

To carry this similarity much further, however, would be naïve and distortive. The reader should not forget that the Greek, Italian, and Polish communities in the United States are separated from their homelands by thousands of miles and exist as small enclaves within a larger foreign culture and society. This is not the case with the Israeli Arabs. Until 1948, they were the majority and the Jews were the minority in the British mandate of Palestine. Today, however, they are the minority in Israel. But Israel itself is considered a small foreign element in an area that is predominantly Arab and primarily Muslim. Thus the parallel between Israeli Arabs as a minority ethnic group and the Greeks or Italians in the United States has significant limitations. In addition to the special nature of the minority-majority relation between Arabs and Jews in Israel, there is the problem of the hostility that exists between Israel and the Arab nations. This hostility has had and continues to have direct repercussions on the acceptance of the Israeli Arab community by the larger Israeli society.

Two of the major repercussions are the exclusion of Israeli Arabs from military service and the fact that they have been and are subject to military rule. As many commentators on Israeli society have observed, the army serves as a major socialization agent. It plays a significant role in transforming Moroccans, Iraqis, Indians, Germans, and Russians into Israelis. It helps them to adopt a more homogeneous style of dress, set of social relationships, interests, friendships, and so on. The Arab community, however, is excluded from this all-important adult socialization experience. Until December of 1966, much of the Arab community was under miliatry law. Arabs who lived in the northern regions (as most of them did) and in the extreme south were required to obtain passes from the military governor when they wished to visit other parts of Israel. Curfews existed or were imposed frequently.

The Israeli Arabs recognize that they hold a peculiar status within Israeli society and within the Middle East. Some express their recognition by refusing to think of themselves as a minority within a Jewish state and identify solely with the Arab majority in the Middle East. Landau, in *The Arabs in Israel* has reported on a symposium held in Jerusalem in 1962. He quotes from a lecture by Salim Jubran (an Israeli Arab):

> How does an Arab see himself in Israel? We the Arabs in Israel were a majority, while the Jews were a minority; it is not so simple to change from being a majority to a minority within a short time . . . The problem of the Arab citizen in Israel is unique. I do not know of any other instance where a national minority exists in an environment surrounded by peoples of the same nation, without a state of peace between them . . . Everyone in the world must support the movement to liberate his own people; one should explain to the Arabs of Israel that loyalty to this State does not clash with the liberation movement of the Arab people. (1969:28-9)

Given these facts — that is, the peculiar minority-majority status of the Arabs in Israel — and the hostility between Israel and the neighboring states, it would be naïve to assess the degree to which the Arab community will become acculturated or remain separate solely on the basis of the desires of the Arabs or the Jews within Israel. Some scholars have suggested that there is a good analogy between the status of the Arabs in Israel and that of the black community in the United States. They claim that although white Americans may not have as realistic a basis for concern about the loyalty of the black community, the scholars nevertheless have questioned whether in periods of crisis they could count on the loyalty of black citizens. Such questions have not been asked about the loyalty of other ethnic communities except when the United States has been at war with the homeland of the people of those communities. Then, as we have seen, all doubts have been resolved in favor of national security, at the cost of depriving civil liberties even to American-born Germans (during World War I) and Japanese (during World War II).

Another similarity between the relationship that Arabs have with the dominant culture in Israel and the place of blacks in white American society is the sense of superiority that members of the larger groups have about themselves and their sense that blacks or Arabs are inferior. Thus the Arab community in Israel must not only resolve its own ambivalence about the quality and the extent of the contact it wants to have with the larger culture, but it must also deal with its own sense of inferiority vis-à-vis the larger culture, and the awareness that most Israelis wish it was not there.[1]

Some, perhaps a major portion, of the tension between the two communities might be resolved if the Arab nations were to recognize the state of Israel and were to engage in diplomatic as well as economic and social relations with it. Then the island-within-an-island existence that the Israeli Arabs experience would disappear, and they would have an opportunity to redefine their status both in terms of Israeli society in particular and the Middle East as a whole.

If the status of the Arab community in Israel is similar in some important ways to that of blacks in the United States, then the status of the ultra-Orthodox Jewish community in Israel might be compared with that of the Black Muslims vis-à-vis the Christian black community, and to that of the Amish, the Mennonites, and the Mormons in the United States. One major similarity between the ultra-Orthodox Jews and the Black Muslims is the sense of superiority that each group feels toward the larger group to which it is connected by history, religion, or skin color but from whom it also feels estranged. The Black Muslims view the black Christians with both contempt and pity — the latter because they perceive them as victims of a slave mentality that the white culture has fostered upon them through their internalization of Christian symbolism. The sense of contempt stems from the belief that the black Christians are too stupid and too passive to realize that they are being duped by whites in the name of Christianity.

In the words of Eric Lincoln:

America's so-called Negroes, say the Muslims, have been kept in mental slavery by the white man, even while their bodies were free. They have been systematically and diabolically estranged from their heritage and from themselves. "They have been educated in ignorance," kept from any knowledge of their origin, history, true names or religion. Reduced to helplessness under the domination of the whites, they are now so lost that they even seek friendship and acceptance from their mortal enemies, rather than from their own people. They are shackled with the names of the Slavemasters; they are duped by the Slavemaster's religion; they are divided and have no language, flag or country of their own. Yet they do not even know enough to be ashamed. (1961:69–70)

Lincoln continues his description of the Black Muslim thesis:

The most unforgivable offense of these so-called Negroes is that they "are guilty of loving the white race and all that that race goes for . . . [for] the white race [is] their arch deceiver." Malcoln X sums up the result of centuries of indoctrination by the white man:

"As 'Negro Christians' we idolized our Christian Slavemaster, and lived for the day when his plurality of white gods would allow us to mingle and mix up with them. We worshipped the false beauty of the Slavemaster's leprous looking women . . . We regarded them with the utmost respect, courtesy and kindness, bowing, and tipping our hats, showing our teeth. We perfected the art of humility and politeness for their sake . . . but at the same time we treated our own women as if they were mere animals, with no love, respect or protection . . .

"We were supposed to be a part of the 'Christian Church,' yet we lived in a bitter world of dejection . . . being rejected by the white 'Christian Church.' In large numbers we became victims of drunkenness, drug addiction, reefer smoking . . . in a false and futile attempt to 'escape' the reality and horror of the shameful condition that the Slavemaster's Christian religion had placed us in . . . Fear ruled us, but not fear of God. We had fear of the Slavemaster, we had no knowledge of truth and we were apparently afraid to let him see us practicing love and unity towards each other.

"Is it a wonder that the world laughed at us and held us [up] to scorn? We practiced love of others, while hating ourselves . . . patience with others and impatience with our own kind . . . unity with others and disunity with our own kind. We called ourselves 'Negro Christians,' yet we remained an ignorant, foolish people, despised and REJECTED by the white Christians. We were fools!" (1961:70)

Lincoln continues:

The Negro's plight was forced upon him by the white man, but it persists because the Negro has been willing to remain "in a land not his own." It can only be solved by separation. So long as Negroes live among whites, they will be subject to the white man's abuse of power — economic and political. Separation will provide the only realistic opportunity for mutual respect between the races. (1961:72).

For the ultra-Orthodox Jewish community in Israel, the desire for separation is just as intense. But it is not from the Christians or Muslims that they wish to remain separated — it is from Zionists, from Israelis, from Jews who belong to the religious parties that have demonstrated their willingness to compromise with secularism. As is described later in this chapter, in the United States the ultra-Orthodox Jews have also maintained themselves as a separate community and have built thick and solid sociological walls in order to protect themselves not only from Christian influence but from what they consider to be the insidious influence of Jewish-American culture as well.

The ultra-Orthodox Jews, like the Black Muslims, also condemn their brethren for prostituting themselves before false gods and for accepting Zionist charity, money, and political benefits. For the ultra-Orthodox, Zionism and not Christianity is the "god" that is responsible for their condition.

Lincoln captures the tone of the Black Muslims with this quote from Malcolm X:

"Your Christian countries, if I am correct, are the countries of Europe and North and South America. Predominantly, this is where you find Christianity, or at least people who represent themselves as Christians. Whether they practice what Jesus taught is something we won't go into. The Christian world is what we usually call the Western world . . . The colonization of the dark people in the rest of the world was done by Christian powers. The number one problem that most people face in the world today is how to get freedom from Christians. Wherever you find non-white people today they are trying to get back their freedom from people who represent themselves as Christians, and if you ask these [subject] people their picture of a Christian, they will tell you 'a white man – a Slavemaster.'" (1961:28)

Lincoln then continues:

Because Christianity is the white man's religion, the repudiation of Christianity is an overt act of aggression against the white man. To be identified with a movement that openly rejects the fundamental values of a powerful majority is to increase vastly one's self-esteem and one's stature among one's peers. (1961:29)

Like the ultra-Orthodox Jews, the Black Muslims also point with pride to the manner in which they handle social problems such as juvenile delinquency, broken homes, promiscuity, drugs, and alcoholism. The Black Muslims claim that they have restored the woman to a place of dignity and respect, "while restoring to the man his traditional responsibilities as head of the family . . . Children seem to profit the most, for among Muslim children, delinquency is unheard of" (Lincoln, 1961:32).

For the ultra-Orthodox, the Jew who thinks he can compromise between a secular and sacred life, between dedication to the Torah and allegiance to the state of Israel, is a hypocrite and a fool. The Black Muslims have a comparable view of the Christian blacks. They claim that "those so called Negroes who seek integration with the American white man are unrealistic and stupid . . . But for the pseudo Negro leaders, to be accepted by whites and to be in their company is worth more than heaven itself. These Negroes are forever begging and licking the white man's boots for [him] to smile and pat [them] on the back" (Lincoln, 1961:88).

The major theme that one finds in the history of immigration to the United States is that within two generations most ethnic communities have become acculturated into the American scene if they were accepted into the larger society. Some groups maintain their own religious institutions; others support their own school systems; some establish newspapers and magazines; but despite all this, the children of Polish, Scandinavian, Italian, Irish, and Greek families in America learn English, play American sports, dress like the other American children, see the same movies, and adopt the heroes of the day. The Chinese and the Japanese are examples of ethnic groups whose acceptance by the larger American society was much more problematic than it was for any European group. They found barriers placed before them to some of the more important institutions in American society. Even today they are less acculturated than any of the other previously named groups.[2]

In addition, however, there have been some communities that were not rejected by the larger American society because of different skin color, religion, or traditions, but who chose to remain apart and maintain a separate existence. These were people who viewed contact with the larger society as dangerous to their moral, material, and cultural well-being. The Amish, the Mennonites, and the Mormons are communities that fit those characteristics most clearly and that have been most successful at maintaining the integrity of their communities.

Writing about the Amish in the United States in 1958, Elmer Lewis Smith has commented:

The Amish sect, unlike many minority groups in America — national, religious or racial — does not seek integration into the total society. They do not seek assimilation, which represents a fusion of the group into the dominant group through attitudes, ideas and social relationships, nor are they interested in any biological amalgamation through intermarriage; in fact, the Amish sect members even fear the process of acculturation, which represents a synthesis of the Amish culture with that of the total American culture.

At best, the Amish seek accommodation, or a state of equilibrium in which working arrangements can be developed whereby they may maintain their unique group life without conflict; in short, they seek a kind of antagonistic cooperation. The Amish group's aim, then, is merely tolerance for their differences, and they are not at all interested in assimilation, "Americanization," or anything that would tend to merge them with the American culture and society.

To maintain their separation from the world, the Amish group members are restricted in their occupational choice, civic participation, residential location and association with non-Amish peoples. These restrictions do, in reverse, what our dominant society does to other minority groups, such as the colored people, when it discriminates against them in work, living areas, social life and even public and civic participation. The Amish, on the other hand, have voluntarily segregated themselves in order to maintain their unique way of life, and to keep it pure. (1958:226–7)

The sense of superiority and specialness that the ultra-Orthodox Jews feel with respect to other Jews is not unlike the beliefs held by the Mormons with respect to the Gentiles. In *Desert Saints*, Nels Anderson wrote:

... the Mormons would never have achieved the status of a "peculiar people" had they not isolated themselves from the Gentiles. Free association with outsiders would have minimized the differences between them and other people. They might have remained in Missouri, but they would not have developed the cultural patterns which still distinguish them from other frontier people.

Pioneers in Zion could hardly have been good Saints without holding Gentiles in contempt. It was their duty to glorify their uninviting habitat, and that was not easy; but it was easier if they could sincerely dislike the Gentiles, who had made their migration necessary. For the Saints, their hate for the Gentiles made easier the obligations for cooperation in economic matters and stimulated appreciation for their social exclusiveness. (1942:420)

Indeed Brigham Young told his people what the ultra-Orthodox Jews believe about themselves: "We are the best people in the world!" The Molokan and the Dukhobor, two Christian sects that came from Russia to the United States and Canada at the beginning of the twentieth century, are examples of communities that were unable to maintain their isolation from the majority culture. In her monograph *The Pilgrims of Russian-Town* Pauline Young decribed what happened to the Molokans after they came to California (between 1905 and 1907) and settled in the heart of Los Angeles.

The struggle of this sect to maintain its existence as a moral and social entity in an environment to which it is utterly strange and alien is perhaps more intense than the struggle of any other immigrant group known to American life. Their life is strange and alien, first of all because the Molokans are Russian; second, because they are a rural people, a people who have lived until recently in an environment in which there were no automobiles, no telephones, no radios, and no newspapers; and finally, because they are a sect, a primitive religious group, who have sought to find somewhere within the limits of a world that is every day growing smaller — and of a political and social order that is growing daily tighter — a place of refuge and escape from that world. (1932:2–3)

Characterizing relations between the older and younger generations, Young wrote:

The Molokan youth display many of the tensions and much of the unrest characteristic of immigrant groups in transition from an older to a newer culture. The youth seem to their parents and to others "to sail in a ship without a rudder"; cut off from the anchorage of habitual modes of action, they drift at the mercy of unknown currents. Their confusion and tensions manifest themselves in disobedience, in disrespect for elders, in delinquency and crime. Such behavior on the part of the children kindles on the part of the elders a more fervent desire to "flee from the wickedness of this world" and to draw the young into the protective walls of sectarianism. The defenses and the struggle of this group against the assimilation of young are numerous and intense. The situation is complex, as a Molokan elder implied when he said: "We are up against it when dealing with the American community, though many of them have become our friends; we are up against it with our own children, and do not have much grace with the newcomers of our old villages." (1932:10)

In her conclusions, she predicts the community's failure to retain the loyalty of its youth.

Since the Molokans no longer face religious persecution and disenfranchisement, the youth feel that there is no necessity for preserving the social uniqueness of the sect, and take a cool, critical attitude toward the "glorious past" of their group. The result is a conflict of cultures between the old and the young, which rages over dress, food, work, leisure, opinions, ideas, and ideals. Almost any attitude, any route of life may precipitate the battle between the old and the new. The equilibrium disturbed, the young generation finds, however, few adequate, adaptive adjustments with which to meet the new conditions of life. Tensions and unrest arise. Life in its very essentials is in an upheaval. The road from the old to the new is uncharted and dangerous at every step. (1932:160)

The ultra-Orthodox Jewish community has succeeded in maintaining its separate and antagonistic status vis-à-vis the larger Israeli society since the establishment of the state in 1948. It did so even though a few years earlier, in 1945, the community witnessed the "surrender" by the leadership of the Agudat Party to the seductive offers of the Zionist movement. The Agudat agreed at that time to join the pregovernment structure and to throw its lot in with the secularists and with the other religious movements that had many years earlier cast their values and symbols into a Zionist mold.

Of course the ultra-Orthodox Jews have had hundreds of years of experience in Central and Eastern Europe in maintaining themselves and protecting their young from being enticed into the Gentile and/or secular Jewish worlds of Warsaw, Berlin, Budapest, and Vienna. For many reasons, however, their task in these settings was easier than that which they confront in modern-day Jerusalem. In Central and Eastern Europe, the larger society was at best indifferent and uninterested in them; and for long periods of time, it was hostile and rejecting. Indeed, it was the larger society that built the physical walls of the ghettos and passed the laws restricting the movements of Jews, their choice of occupations, and their access to educational institutions. It is only recently, perhaps since the end of World War I and in some parts of the world not until World War II, that the physical walls were torn down and the legal restrictions rescinded. Today in Israel and in the United States the ultra-Orthodox community has built sociological walls that appear to be as effective and as restrictive as any of the stone walls that had been built in earlier times by the dominant groups.

There have been two recent studies of the ultra-Orthodox community in a section of Brooklyn known as Williamsburg.[3] Like the ultra-Orthodox community in Israel, the Hasidim of Williamsburg have worked to isolate themselves not only from non-Jews and nonreligious Jews, but also from religious Orthodox Jews, whose ideology, fervor, and observance of traditional religious practices do not meet Hasidic standards. According to Poll, "the main object of this group is to maintain itself in isolation. These Hasidim are primarily concerned with their own religiosity — they are neither interested nor are they anxious to persuade other Jews to subscribe to their way of life through direct contact with them" (1969:viii). The Hasidic community in Williamsburg is composed mainly of people who survived the Holocaust and who decided to leave Hungary and some other parts of Eastern Europe and emigrate to the United States. As of 1959, its estimated size was about 12,000. Like the community in Mea Shearim, the street language in Williamsburg is mainly Yiddish, with some Hungarian and English. Poll compares the Hasidic community to the Mennonites, Hutterites, and Amish in the following manner:

There are certain features common to these groups and to the Hasidim. All of them are religious minorities. They all attempt to isolate themselves socially from the larger community in order to maintain their own group norms and values. Their fear of loss of group identification, of assimilation into the larger groups around them, and of the gradual breakdown of group values makes such isolation a seeming necessity. Some try to maintain group identification over their members by establishing insular economies. These methods of control are shared by most of the groups, including the Hasidim.

However, the Hasidim differ markedly from the other groups in several respects. Most of these groups are agricultural, but the Hasidim are not. Whereas most of these groups live in physical isolation, away from urban industrial areas, the Hasidim live in the middle of a metropolis. Whereas the Hutterites produce a great number of items for their own consumption, the Hasidim purchase all raw materials outside the community, some of which they process and transform in "Hasidic goods" so that these goods can receive the sanction of the group . . . Whereas the Amish, who are "seeking to maintain a way of life similar to that of their martyr forefathers, must consciously seek to resist the new innovations that are continually offered through science and technology," the Hasidim use such innovations in ways in which they do not necessarily become a threat to group cohesion. The Hasidim have been able to employ technology in economic activities that not only do not require violation of religious laws but that actually complement and supplement religious observance while providing an acceptable living for individual community members and economic support for the community's religious activities.

Furthermore, there is a non-Hasidic Jewish community between the Hasidim and the non-Jewish community serving as a "social wall" to deflect the values of the outside world before they can penetrate to the Hasidim. Finally, the identification with the group is much stronger among the Hasidim than among other groups. Hasidic group cohesion is much more dependent upon internal identity than upon outside pressures forcing solidarity. As a matter of fact, the Hasidim form a cohesive community in which the cultural goals and the institutionalized norms operate jointly and effectively in shaping economic practices. (1969:10–11)

The daily regimen among the Hasidim in Williamsburg is very much like the daily routine among residents of Jerusalem, Manchester, and in any other part of the world they happen to be. The men spend most of their time in houses of prayer, learning, praying, and gossiping. The woman look after their homes, their children (on the average of six per family), and do the necessary shopping. The children attend school from the early morning until the evening. Attendance at or participation in sports, music, and other recreational or artistic activities is not part of the life style of this community. Television sets, even radios, are taboo, because "it brings into the house those sounds and voices which are not conducive to the worship of God." Reading Yiddish newspapers is also discouraged because "the editors are unsympathetic towards the Hasidic Jews and spread lies about them" and because "the Yiddish papers are published on the Sabbath, too, and what can a religious Jew expect from desecrators of the holy Sabbath?" (Poll, 1969:32).

Because the community in Williamsburg, like the one in Mea Shearim is not surrounded by hostile forces, nor does it have the physical wall of a ghetto to protect it, the leaders continually exhort their people to resist Americanization or Israelization. For example, Poll reports that:

When the Hasidim travel on the subways and trains or walk on the streets, they observe behavior that is not conducive to adherence to rigid Hasidic standards. Therefore, the Hasidim are warned by their leaders to avoid traveling on overcrowded trains, since these trains are "full of dissolute women who are half-naked."

It is much better, they are told, to change their jobs and work in close proximity to the Hasidic community so that they will not be exposed to sights that might have a deterrent effect on their prescribed Hasidic observances. It is better to earn less money than to work with nonreligious people and "listen to their idle talk and watch their manners." But since it is impossible for many Hasidim to stay within the community and earn a living, they inevitably meet people whose behavior is not acceptable and from whom they may learn the patterns of the general culture. To counteract this bad influence, these Hasidim are bidden to study every day before work and after work to confirm their faith and to strengthen their Hasidic behavior. (1969:49—50)

Rubin, in his 1972 study of the Williamsburg community, addressed himself specifically to the issue of how Satmar (a Hasidic group that is very isolationist and anti-Israel and whose followers make up much of the membership of the Naturei Karta) manages to keep its American-born and bred youngsters from leaving the community for the opportunities offered by living in New York City.

Rubin's observations led him to conclude that the community exerted four interrelated types of controls: (1) prevention or removal of temptation, (2) reward, (3) socialization, and (4) external reinforcement. Examples of how temptations are withdrawn occur in areas such as sexual behavior and food. For example, boys and girls are separated from the time they are at least three years old. They attend separate schools, and they do not meet in play groups, sports, or artistic endeavor. Teenagers are answerable to their elders for their whereabouts at all times.

On the matter of rewards, the community offers a wide variety covering emotional, social, and financial needs. For example, when prospective mothers go to the hospital to have their babies, neighbors assume responsibility for the children who are at home and for the husband; when there is sickness, there is volunteer nursing on a regular basis. Joyous occasions such as weddings or Bar Mitzvahs are community celebrations; and if families have financial difficulties, they can assume that the local yeshiva, loan fund, or charitable organization will provide. According to Rubin, the key to the social control system is the socialization process.

In Satmar there are no double standards, so often observed and commented upon in the larger American culture. No significant adult reserves for himself the right to violate norms that he wishes to inculcate in the young. Likewise, matters of belief are discussed in a way that takes basic postulates for granted. Theologizing that would tend to raise doubts is totally omitted. Thus a growing youngster encounters no contradiction in the behavior of significant adults to the world view that he is being taught. (1972:192)

On the matter of external reinforcement, the Satmar community has many opportunities to compare itself with other communities and show how it has succeeded in achieving adherence to values that other groups share but fail to attain. For example, most Jewish groups oppose "mixed marriage". Yet it occurs — but not among the Satmar. Crime, juvenile delinquency, illegitimacy, and other undesirable behavior are found in other groups who share the same negative values concerning them. They are almost nonexistent within the Satmar community.

Rubin concluded his study with the following observation:

In sum, Satmar safeguards its core culture and controls against deviation by minimizing opportunities to deviate, by offering the obedient rewards which are withheld from the deviant, by its socialization system that not only inculcates the "right" way of living but also teaches one how to enjoy the rewards and, more important, prevents the acquisition of mental tools that might enable one to seek and find alternative satisfactions. And many aspects of the world without reinforce the Satmarer's definition of the world, thus diminishing the likelihood of their renouncing their own culture. (1972:195)

This chapter, then, has placed the Israeli Arabs and the ultra-Orthodox Jewish communities within larger geographical and theoretical settings. It has shown that the situation of the Arab community resembles both that of the European ethnic communities that came to the United States in the nineteenth century and that of American blacks. The Israeli Arabs are comparable to the former in that many of their members, especially those born in Israel, have adopted the language, the styles of dress, and the leisure activities of the larger group and have availed themselves of the educational and economic opportunities found in the larger society. Like American blacks, they are perceived by the larger group as inferior and undesirable.

The ultra-Orthodox Jewish community, on the other hand, is most aptly compared with the Black Muslims and to Protestants sects such as the Amish, the Mormons, and the Mennonites. Just as the Black Muslims feel disdain and contempt for other blacks, especially black Christians, so do the ultra-Orthodox Jews disapprove of the practices of other Jews (especially those who claim they are Orthodox). Their similarity with the Mormons and the Amish stems from their insistence on social isolation and autonomy.

2. Social characteristics and research design

This chapter describes the social and demographic characteristics of the ultra-Orthodox Jewish and the urban Arab communities. The research plan and the obstacles encountered in gaining access to the ultra-Orthodox community are reported. The first few pages serve to locate the two communities within the sociopolitical context of the larger society.

The modern state of Israel was officially established on May 14, 1948. It was a country composed of 650,000 Jews who had come mostly from Central and Eastern Europe, and 700,000 Arabs. By the time the fighting that had begun just after the UN resolution in favor of partition ended in 1949, the Arab population was reduced to 156,000. Today there are almost 3,000,000 Jews in Israel and about 425,000 Arabs.[1] The characteristics of the Jewish population changed greatly as a result of immigration. The majority of Israelis today come from or have parents who were born in other parts of the Middle East, Asia, and Africa.

While Oriental Jews (Jews from Asia, Africa, and the Middle East) are in the majority, political, economic, and social power still remains within the control of the European Ashkenazi community. Until 1974 when Itzhak Rabin became prime minister, all of the former heads of state had been born in Eastern Europe, whence Rabin's family also comes. Almost all of the other important political posts have been and still are occupied by Israelis of European background. European Jews enjoy higher incomes and educational and occupational statuses than do Jews from Africa and Asia. Tables 2.1 and 2.2 demonstrate those differences.

Table 2.2 describes occupational characteristics by Jewish ethnic communities. The statistics show that almost half of the men born in Europe and America have white-collar occupations, in contrast to less than a quarter of those born in Asia and Africa. The proportion of farmers is larger among the Asian-Africans, and so is the proportion of blue-collar workers (approximately two-thirds against one-half). Those born in Israel also have a comparatively higher share of the professional and technical positions.

Since the founding of the state, one of the main centers of elitism in Israel has been the kibbutz movement. Many of the current political leaders, members of the diplomatic corps, and generals in the army spent some part of their lives on a kibbutz, even though kibbutz dwellers represent less than 10 percent of the Israeli population. There

Table 2.1. *Average gross annual money income per employee's family,
by continent of birth and period of immigration of family head (1971)*

Continent of birth and period of immigration of family head	Gross income (Israeli pounds)	Years of education of family head	Average size of family	Percentage of families, by continent and immigration
Total	12,800	9.9	4.0	100.0
Jew	12,900	10.0	3.9	97.2
Asia-Africa, total	10,700	8.1	4.8	40.3
Immigrated:				
Up to 1947	11,900	8.3	4.2	4.6
1948−54	11,500	8.4	4.9	21.6
1955−60	9,800	8.0	4.9	6.9
Since 1961	8,500	7.0	4.9	7.2
Europe-America, total	14,400	10.9	3.2	41.4
Immigrated:				
Up to 1947	16,100	12.1	5.3	14.2
1948−54	14,900	10.2	3.3	15.5
1955−60	12,900	10.6	3.0	4.5
Since 1961	11,000	10.6	2.8	7.2
Israel born, total	14,600	12.3	3.7	15.5
Fathers born in:				
Asia-Africa	11,100	9.3	4.1	3.3
Europe-America	16,300	14.0	3.5	8.8
Israel	13,600	10.9	3.7	3.4
Non-Jews	8,600	6.4	6.4	2.8

Source: Curtis, 1973:207.

Table 2.2. *Jewish employed men by occupation, place of birth, and period of immigration, 1969 (percentages)*

Major occupation	Total Jews	Born in Israel	Born in Asia and Africa					Born in Europe and America				
			Total	Prior to 1947	1948–1954	1955–1960	1961 and after	Total	Prior to 1947	1948–1954	1955–1960	1961 and after
Professional, scientific, technical	11.4	16.9	5.7	7.5	5.7	4.2	6.1	13.7	14.2	11.3	19.9	15.3
Administrative, executive, managerial, clerical	16.4	15.6	9.5	10.8	10.1	9.5	5.8	22.7	30.3	19.7	14.0	13.0
Traders, agents, sales persons	8.2	4.7	7.9	12.5	8.7	4.4	5.5	10.0	10.6	11.0	7.1	6.6
All white-collar workers	36.0	37.2	23.1	30.8	24.5	18.1	17.4	46.4	55.1	42.0	41.0	34.9
Farmers, fishers	9.0	10.8	10.8	7.0	10.6	14.0	10.4	6.6	6.9	6.3	6.6	6.9
All blue-collar workers	55.0	52.0	66.1	62.2	65.9	67.9	72.2	47.0	38.0	51.7	52.4	58.2
Workers in transportation and communication	7.4	10.8	6.4	11.3	7.0	4.7	2.7	6.6	7.0	8.3	3.7	2.1
Construction workers, miners	8.7	5.6	13.1	10.4	14.4	12.4	10.6	6.3	6.3	6.7	5.4	5.7
Craftsmen, production process	30.3	31.6	33.7	26.0	32.1	35.9	43.6	26.9	20.2	27.9	34.5	41.3
Services, sports, entertainment	8.6	4.0	12.9	14.5	11.4	14.9	15.3	7.2	4.5	8.8	8.8	9.1
Total (%)	100.0	100.0	100.0	100.0	100.0	100.0	100.0	100.0	100.0	100.0	100.0	100.0
Total (X1,000)	591.6	117.2	215.8	24.2	123.3	38.8	29.5	258.6	103.3	101.7	25.7	27.9

Source: Labor Force Surveys of the Israeli Central Bureau of Statistics, *Statistical Abstract* No. 21, (1970a:280–1).

have been and there are today no kibbutzim that were founded by Jews who emigrated to Israel from Morocco, India, Tunisia, or other parts of Africa and Asia.

In most parts of Israel the Oriental and European communities are segregated; their children do not attend the same elementary schools, and the adults do not share the same shops or places of recreation. The separatism is a function of wealth; it has no basis in law. South Tel Aviv, for example, which has slums and commerce and industry, is largely Oriental, while North Tel Aviv, which has the university and fashionable shops and restaurants, is largely European. The percentage of intermarriage between the two communities reached a high point of 17.5 percent in 1969.

Since 1970, protest groups composed largely of younger members of the Oriental Jewish community who live in the slums of Tel Aviv have become more visible and more impatient for change. The name that the loudest and largest of these groups chose is the Black Panthers. Their activities include demonstrations, picketing, sit-ins, especially at the ministry of housing, and at the Knesset.

Shlomo Avineri, one of Israel's foremost political scientists and currently director general of the Ministry of Foreign Affairs, has compared the status of the Oriental Jews to that of the Italian and the Irish communities in the United States at an earlier period.

The integration of the Oriental immigrant into the political structure of Israeli life thus shows remarkable similarities with the process through which Irish and Italian (and Jewish) immigrants became integrated into the American political structure at the turn of the century. None of the political alienation and exclusion which until very recently characterized the position of the American blacks can be found in the process which the Oriental communities are undergoing in Israel. Like the Italians and the Irish in America, they still are at the bottom of the economic ladder – though . . . they are moving up quite rapidly. It would be foolish to deny that there still exist many popular prejudices and generalizations about the Oriental immigrants – but these exist even with regard to non-WASP white Christian groups in the United States. But if one looks for American parallels, it is among the Italian and the Irish that one would find something akin to the position of the Oriental communities in Israel – not among the blacks. (1973:293)

Avineri has concluded:

The present challenge of integrating the Oriental communities is not a new one. The recent outbursts only pinpoint those areas where it had misfired, and not its overall failure. With the takeover of local politics by the Oriental communities, with the economic gaps generally narrowing between Westerns and Orientals, the structure of Israeli society is definitely changing in the direction of further integration of the non-Western groups. That the process is not easy, that one tends now more than ever to see Israel as it is, warts and all, is a measure of Israel's growing normalcy. That Israel has to set its eyes on much higher achievements, and that it is responding to the internal challenges just as to the external ones, is a measure of the vitality of its social vision. (1973:304)

In addition to the Oriental and European Jews and the Arabs (about 75 percent of whom are Muslim, and almost all of the rest are Roman and Greek Catholics), Israel has several other much smaller communities such as the Druze, the Samaritans, and the Circassians. Of these, the Druze is the largest, containing about 35,000 members. The Druze live almost exclusively in the northern region and are engaged mainly in farming.

As indicated in the Introduction, we selected the ultra-Orthodox Jews and the Arabs for study because of the important and distinctive roles they have played and are likely to play in defining the quality and the characteristics of Israeli society as a whole. The selection of the Arab community needs much less elaboration. The Arabs are the largest minority in the country. They have strong ties to the other countries in the Middle East, most of whom have been officially in a state of war with Israel since its establishment. They belong to a different religion, speak a different language, and have a different history, traditions, and customs. It was thus almost obligatory to select the Arab community for study if one wanted to provide some insights into how Israeli society is likely to define itself in the next generation.

The ultra-Orthodox Jewish community is among the smaller communities in Israel, representing at most 55,000 people (if one includes people who support the Agudat Party and those who refuse to support even the most Orthodox of the religious parties because they do not accept the legitimacy of the state). But small as the population is, members of the ultra-Orthodox grouping exercise a distinctive and large influence on the character of the society. And perhaps most important of all, even though they share with the majority a common religion, language, and much of the same history and tradition, they have set themselves apart. In their separateness they have also established a moral hierarchy in which they place themselves at the top. These people view their values, life style, and institutions as superior to all others and as more likely and more worthy of survival. They believe that they have been chosen for a special kind of existence. For all of these reasons, I believe that this community of ultra-Orthodox Jews will maintain its distinctiveness, will remain culturally and socially intact, and will resist acculturation, assimilation, or integration more successfully than the larger ethnic communities. In doing so, it will contrive to act as a thorn in the side of the other religious parties and of the society as a whole.

The next section provides a brief description of the social structure and demographic characteristics of the two ethnic communities. The final section describes the methods employed in collecting and analyzing the data collected in the surveys and the obstacles encountered, especially during the early stages of the field work.

Mea Shearim: the ultra-Orthodox Jewish community

The ultra-Orthodox respondents live in a neighborhood in the northern section of Jerusalem known as Mea Shearim. The community was founded in 1873 by Orthodox, primarily Hasidic, Jews from Eastern Europe. At the time of its founding, it was the largest Jewish settlement in Jerusalem outside the walls of the Old City.

Today, Mea Shearim is a self-imposed ghetto. Its inhabitants often refer to their neighborhood as the "Jewish Section" of Jerusalem. A walk through the place quickly establishes the distinctive qualities of the neighborhood. The area is a maze of twisting narrow alleys made up of row after row of two- and three-story stone multidwelling apartment buildings, many of which have outside wooden staircases and wooden or metal balconies. Stores, of the small "mom-and-pop" variety, are usually on the street level, with apartments next door or immediately above. In addition to the fruit and vegetable, meat and fish, and dairy markets, some stores specialize in selling sacred books and ritual articles; there are also craft shops where furniture and other household goods are made and sold. Almost every block has at least one synagogue plus a variety of religious schools that are under the aegis of various Hasidic sects or the Agudat Party. There are talmud torahs and yeshivas for boys and men, private schools for girls, and kindergarten and nursery schools for young children.

Unlike other neighbourhoods in Jerusalem, the street language is primarily Yiddish, not Hebrew. The style of dress is also distinctive. The women's skirts are at least "midi" in length; the blouses have long sleeves, and the outfits are subdued in color, and loose fitting. If they are married, the women cover their shaven heads with wigs or wear kerchiefs. Women of all ages, including children of two and three years of age, wear heavy stockings, even in the summer. Shorts or slacks are not worn by girls in school or by their younger and older sisters. Signs are prominantly displayed in various locations throughout the neighborhood warning and exhorting Jewish women about their appearance. One sign that is permanently displayed in the main market reads as follows: "Our torah requires Jewish women to be attired in modest dress, sleeves reaching below the elbows, stockings, married women having their hair cropped . . . are the virtues of the Jewish women throughout the ages."

The men also have a distinctive style of dress. Many wear a garment that is reminiscent of their Hasidic forebears, with long black caftan topcoats and wide-brimmed black hats. Instead of pants many wear knickers with either white or black stockings. Their hairstyle is distinctive by the presence of long side curls and beards.

The 1970 census reported that there are 5,570 inhabitants in Mea Shearim, 5,310 of whom live in households, the other 260 being located in institutions in the community. In total the census reports 1,386 households in Mea Shearim. Forty-nine percent of the inhabitants are women, and 51 percent are men. An image popularly held in Israel is that Mea Shearim is a "dying community," that it is a community inhabited largely by elderly people whose children have moved away and one to which younger people are not attracted. But this image is not supported by the census data (presented in Table 2.3) which show the following age distribution for the residents of Mea Shearim: Ten percent of the inhabitants are sixty-five and older; but 62 percent are less than thirty-five.

Thirty percent of the residents are foreign born. Among the foreign born, slightly over one-half arrived before the establishment of the state in 1948; almost all of the rest came between 1948 and 1951. This later cohort was made up largely of inmates from the displaced persons' camps that were established after World War II for survivors of the concentration camps.[2]

Marriage occurs at an earlier age among the members of this community than it does for the rest of the Jewish Israeli population. The girls usually have their husbands selected for them, are married, and have had their first child by the time they are twenty-one. Their husbands are usually under twenty-five.

Table 2.3. *Age distribution for residents of Mea Shearim*

Distribution in years	Number of people	Cumulative (%)
0—4	650	11.7
5—9	699	24.2
10—14	621	35.3
15—19	522	44.6
20—24	427	52.2
25—29	302	57.6
30—34	267	62.3
35—44	425	69.9
45—54	522	79.2
55—64	589	89.7
65—74	361	96.1
75+	185	100.0

The community's educational level is much higher than the national average, especially among the male population. Almost all of the men in Mea Shearim attend school past the equivalent of the twelfth grade. Among the rest of the society, about 60 percent complete secondary school. Over 90 percent of the children in Mea Shearim attend elementary or secondary schools that are either under the supervision of the Agudat Party or that are totally independent of the state or of any religious movement affiliated with the state. Schools in this latter category include yeshivas, talmud torahs, nursery schools and kindergartens, elementary and secondary schools, and teaching seminaries for girls. They are supervised, financed, and staffed by various Hasidic communities that have followers and supporters in the United States, Great Britain, Australia, and in other parts of the world. The language of instruction in these independent schools is Yiddish, not Hebrew. The Agudat network receives state funding, but little in the way of curriculum supervision. The language of instruction in the Agudat schools in Hebrew.[3]

Unlike young Jewish males in every other section of Israeli society, the young men in Mea Shearim who attend the yeshivas (and almost all of them do) are exempt from military service.

Those heads of households who are gainfully employed (that is, those who do not devote their full time to prayer, or study at the yeshivas) work mainly as shopkeepers, artisans, or as clerks in the post office or other government agencies. Unlike a high proportion of other Israeli Jewish women, most of the married women in Mea Shearim do not work outside their homes.

Arabs in urban centers[4]

Israeli Arabs comprise about 13 percent of the total population,[5] with about two-thirds living in rural areas and one-third in urban centers. Those who live in the urban centers are concentrated almost wholly in the five cities from which our sample of Arab respondents was selected: Acco, Haifa, Jaffa, Lod, and Ramle.[6] Table 2.4 describes the Arab and Jewish population in those cities.

Approximately 75 percent of the Israeli Arabs are Muslims; the rest are Christians, mostly Greek Catholics, and Greek Orthodox and Latin (Roman) Catholics. Israeli Arabs have among the highest birth rates in the world: 45 per 1,000. The mean number of children per family in the Arab community is 5.0, compared with 2.9 among the Jews. The death rate has dropped to 6 per 1,000, which is approximately one-third of what it was at the end of the British mandate period. The average age of marriage is 25.3 years for Arab men who are Muslims and 20.6 years for Arab Muslim women. This is younger than it is for Jewish men (27.6 years) and women (23.8 years) and also for the Christian Arabs (men, 29.6 years; women 23.2 years), even though in traditional Muslim families the future husband is expected to pay "a bride's price" to his intended's father.

Table 2.4. *Jewish–Arab population distribution in five cities*

City	Jewish	Arab
Acco	33,500	8,700
Haifa	214,500	12,600
Jaffa[a]	382,900	6,900
Lod	28,000	2,900
Ramle	29,000	3,500

[a]The figures represent the population of Tel Aviv and Jaffa combined.
Sources: Statistical Abstract of Israel, 1970, Table B/4 (1970a: 26–7).

According to the 1961 census, 48.3 percent of the Arab population was literate and 50.5 percent had attended school at some time. The differences by sex and age were great; 68 percent of the males were literate and had had some schooling, compared with 28.5 percent of the women. Sixty-four percent of those between fourteen and twenty-nine years of age attended school and were literate, compared with 30 percent in the over-forty-five-years-old category. Since the establishment of the state, the proportion of Arabs who were enrolled in schools increased more than five times. This fivefold increase is significant, even after taking into account the 58 percent increase that occurred in Arab population over the same period.

Table 2.5 describes the median years of schooling, according to the 1961 census, for Arab males and females in the cities from which our sample was drawn.

Some of the gap between the Arab men and women has been narrowed in the decade or so since the 1961 census; but the differences between the Arab and Jewish populations are still large, especially between Arab and Jewish women.

The occupational distributions among Israeli Arabs are described in Table 2.6. Note first the proportion of Arab men and women in the labor force in the five cities. The differences between Arab and Jewish men are relatively small. But Arab women are less likely to be in the labor force than are Jewish women except for the Arab women in Jaffa.

Table 2.5. *Median years of study for Arabs and Jews by city and sex*

| City | Median years of study among population 14 years and over | | | |
| | Arabs | | Jews | |
	Males	Females	Males	Females
Acco	4.5	0.8	7.9	7.3
Haifa	7.5	6.1	9.6	8.9
Jaffa	6.6	5.2	9.2	8.7
Lod	7.2	0.9	7.5	6.8
Ramle	5.6	5.3	7.4	5.8

Source: Central Bureau of Statistics (1966:171).

Table 2.6. *Percentage of Arabs and Jews in the labor force by city and sex*

	Proportion in the labor force			
	Arabs		Jews	
City	Males	Females	Males	Females
Acco	71.9	10.6	66.9	19.4
Haifa	79.6	16.4	77.9	26.8
Jaffa	83.5	29.5	77.0	26.5
Lod	76.4	7.3	78.3	17.3
Ramle	72.0	8.3	77.1	16.1

Source: Central Bureau of Statistics (1966:171).

Table 2.7 compares the distribution of Arab and Jewish participants in the labor force by the types of industry in which they are employed in each of the five cities. The major difference among Arab workers in the five cities is that a much higher proportion of them are found in agriculture in Acco, Lod, and Ramle, rather than in the larger industrial and commercial centers of Haifa and Jaffa. The distribution across industries in Haifa and Jaffa is similar for Arabs and Jews. In both cities Jews are somewhat more represented in commerce and banking; Arabs, in manufacturing industries.

In his article "Social and Political Changes in Arab Society in Israel," Aharon Layish concludes:

Arab society in Israel is in a transition stage. Its traditional structure, though cracks are appearing in it, has not yet collapsed. The intensity of change is not equal in all parts of the social fabric. In view of the uncertainty of political development in the region, especially since the war of October 1973, it is too early to assess the future. (1975:86)

As I have stated earlier, one of the functions of this work is to assess the future: the future at least in terms of determining the nature of the relationship between the Arab communities in the urban centers and the rest of Israeli society.

The research plan

Although they are not unique, the survey data that have been collected from respondents living in Mea Shearim represent one of the rare

Table 2.7. *Percentage of Arabs (A) and Jews (J) in different types of industries by city*

| | City | | | | | | | | | |
| | Acco | | Haifa | | Jaffa | | Lod | | Ramle | |
Type of industry	A	J	A	J	A	J	A	J	A	J
Agriculture	23	4	2	1	5	1	34	2	30	5
Manufacturing	22	40	34	23	36	30	24	37	22	31
Construction	12	7	16	8	7	7	5	8	9	12
Commerce, banking	4	9	11	17	10	20	18	11	3	14
Transport, communication	4	3	9	14	10	7	9	14	7	7
Services	31	36	26	33	31	32	10	26	29	28
Other	3	1	2	4	1	3	–	2	–	3

Source: Central Bureau of Statistics (1966:94).

occasions when members of an ultra-Orthodox community anywhere in the world have been willing to cooperate in a study of that community. As we have seen in Chapter 1, Poll and Rubin conducted sociological studies in Williamsburg, Brooklyn, and there may have been a few others. The fact that both Poll and Rubin had been born in Eastern Europe, and were themselves members of the ultra-Orthodox Hasidic movement earlier in their lives, made their acceptance somewhat less problematic than my own. But as I indicate a few pages hence in discussing the obstacles that were encountered and had to be overcome, the fact that I was an outsider may have helped rather than hindered me in gaining access to these people.

The sample frame for the Jewish respondents was the neighborhood of Mea Shearim as designated by the Israeli census. Once having determined the area's boundaries, interviewers working in teams of two knocked at the door of every dwelling (J) in the neighborhood in order to locate families that had the appropriate characteristics: a son or daughter between the ages of sixteen and twenty-one. The sample frame for the Arab respondents was obtained primarily from elementary school registration lists that were several years old, and secondarily from membership lists in Arab communal organizations.

The reasons for using different techniques in order to generate a sample for each community were due primarily to the differences in the sizes, concentration, and availability of inclusive lists within each community. Since the urban Arab community is larger and more diffuse than the ultra-Orthodox Jewish community, we wanted our sampling procedure to capture and reflect those differences. We decided, therefore, to conduct interviews in all five cities rather than concentrate on one or two. In some of the cities – Haifa, for example – most of the Arab children attend public schools, whereas in the other cities higher proportions attend private schools. To increase the exhaustiveness of the sample frame, we consolidated names and addresses of Muslim Arab families from the lists of as many organizations as possible, along with names obtained from the schools.

Since many of the children in Mea Shearim do not attend schools that are supervised by the state, it would have made no sense to use a comparable sample frame, and the private schools either did not have or would not provide us a list of their former students. Also, since the neighborhood was of a size and concentration that would allow two teams of interviewers working over a period of several months to contact every potential respondent, a list of the families that met our requirements was not as essential. It would, however, have made the job simpler. Later in this chapter there is a fuller discussion of the problem encountered in the collection of the data and in gaining the cooperation of respondents in Mea Shearim.

Within each community, women interviewed mothers and daughters, and men interviewed fathers and sons. Arab interviewers were employed for the Arab survey, and Jewish interviewers, but not persons who were themselves ultra-Orthodox, worked in Mea Shearim. The interviewers worked as a team. While one interviewed the parent, the other interviewed the son or the daughter. This technique not only saved time, but it increased the likelihood of obtaining and completing interviews with both members of the family. It also helped to ensure privacy, especially for the interviews that were conducted with the sons and daughters. On those occasions when the two interviews could not be conducted simultaneously, maintaining privacy for the daughter's interview often posed a problem in Mea Shearim. Sometimes the interviewer was forced to terminate the interview because the parent refused to grant the conditions of privacy that were agreed upon initially.

Obstacles encountered in the collection of data

The residents of Mea Shearim have maintained a long-standing repugnance and resistance to "outside" interference or "meddling" with their way of life. The presence of interviewers, whether they be census takers, tax assessors, social workers, or social researchers, is considered to be one kind of meddling and interference to which they are opposed. Some of the members of this community claim that they can trace the basis for their objections to surveys and interviews to the Bible. They refer to the warnings of the prophets against cooperation with census takers in the reign of King David. Paraphrased in contemporary parlance, the prophets' warnings to the populace about the dangers of providing a government or a ruler with detailed information about how much wealth a citizen has acquired, or the number of children he or she has, are considered by the ultra-Orthodox to be as applicable today as they were three thousand years ago.

In more recent periods, the residents cite instances in which European Jewish communities in the Middle Ages and in the eighteenth and nineteenth centuries suffered economically and physically as a result of information obtained about the demographic characteristics of their communities. During the mandate period under Great Britain, the residents of Mea Shearim successfully resisted British attempts at collecting census-type data.

The fact that at the present time the government is in the hands of Jews has done little to modify the attitudes and behaviors of most of the residents of this community on the issue of cooperation with social surveyors. Before each census, government officials endeavor to gain the cooperation of some of the leaders of the Agudat Party and ask them to act as spokesmen or interpreters to the residents of Mea Shearim. These spokesmen are expected to explain the importance of the census and of the uses made of the information that is collected. They are also expected to allay the community's doubts and fears concerning other uses to which the information might be put. Although cooperation is still below that found in other sections of Jerusalem, those in charge of the data collection feel that they can obtain sufficient information from which to draw reasonably sound conclusions, at least about the characteristics of those families who support the Agudat Party.

But within Mea Shearim there also exist pockets of people who do not recognize the legitimacy of the state or any of its institutions, including the religious parties. These people, many of whom affiliate themselves with the Naturei Karta, which is a very small socio-political-religious movement, do not recognize the legitimacy of the state. Its followers do not vote, do not pay taxes, do not serve in the army, and do not carry the identity cards that every adult citizen in Israel is expected to have in his possession at all times. Neither do they cooperate with census takers or indeed with any representatives of the government.

The Naturei Karta grant that there is nothing inherently evil in a state — "indeed statehood may mean happiness to any other people — but we Jews have been destined for a higher and an essentially different purpose . . . It manifestly is absurd to believe that we have been waiting two thousand years in so much anguish, with so high hopes and with so many heartfelt prayers merely in order to finish up by playing the same role in the world as an Albania or a Honduras." The basic goal of Jewish survival must be bound up with a supernatural plan, part of whose wisdom has been revealed through the Torah with the laws which provide Israel with the technique for "penetrating deeper and further into the treasures of holiness." The Jewish state which has been established not only ignores this purpose but militantly works against it, in the opinion of the Naturei Karta. (Weiner, 1961:150)

Since the followers of Naturei Karta have retained an even greater degree of insulation from the mainstream of Israeli society than have supporters of the Agudat Party, gaining access to them was of course crucial to the purposes of this survey.

Because of the characteristics of this community and of the obstacles that were likely to be encountered in the field, one of the biggest jobs was that of finding skilled, sensitive, and tenacious interviewers.[7] After an extensive search that involved interviewing almost 200 candidates and testing many of them in the field, I organized a staff of six people, two women and four men, who were able to do the job.

The women were students studying sociology at Hebrew University. Both were in their early thirties, one of Yemenite, the other of Eastern European origin. The latter had considerable knowledge about the culture of her potential respondents and could carry on simple conversations in Yiddish. She had also had considerable experience as an interviewer. In her manner, her style of dress, and her obvious familiarity with many aspects of the respondents' culture (which the respondents picked up from her name and the introductory small talk that almost always preceded the interview) she did not threaten them by appearing as the "typical" native-born Israeli woman who they believe dresses and behaves indecently. These personal characteristics, plus extensive field research experience, and an inordinate amount of persistence (motivated by a very strong need for money) made the success of this interviewer understandable.

More difficult to explain is the relative success of the other woman, whose family had come from Yemen. Although she dressed in a style appropriate to Mea Shearim, her appearance indicated that she was an outsider. Her skin, hair color, and features did not resemble those of the women in Mea Shearim. She knew no Yiddish and had little familiarity with the culture of her respondents. (She did come from a family in which there were elements of traditional Judaism, but the traditions were cast in the setting of the Middle East.) Her prior experience as an interviewer, which was also extensive, and her persistence (motivated similarly by financial need), plus the fact that she aroused some sense of curiosity in her respondents, may be sufficient to explain her success. The women questioned Yael about her background much more than they did Hermona. Her "difference," combined with her professional skills and persistence, worked in favor of the study.

On the whole, the women respondents were more willing to be interviewed than the men and were less likely to terminate an interview once it had begun.[8] In a few instances, the mother was willing to be interviewed, but refused to have her daughter interviewed, or insisted that she be present during the interview, or that she be permitted to ask her daughter the questions on the interview schedule. There were no instances in which, once the mother had agreed to the interview, the daughter refused.[9] In those instances in which the mother or father refused to permit the daughter to be interviewed, the typical objection was that the experience itself, irrespective of the content of the interview, would arouse curiosity and questions that would be unhealthy.

Gaining the cooperation of the men in Mea Shearim was more difficult; and therefore the task of finding interviewers who were able and willing to do the job was more difficult. The team that finally worked was composed of four students at Hebrew University, all of whom shared the common characteristics of having been born in Eastern Europe, of having emigrated with their parents to Latin America before they were in their teens, and of having lived in Latin America until they were in their early twenties. Each of them had immigrated to Israel alone, without their families who opted to remain in Latin America. All of them shared a common feeling of isolation from what they perceived to be the mainstream of Israeli society and from Hebrew University student culture. None thought of themselves as "orthodox" or observant of traditional Jewish religious practices. All of them spoke Yiddish. There was no occasion, however, in which the interviews could not be conducted in Hebrew, since all of the men spoke, understood, and were willing to use Hebrew.

Among the male respondents, the father's consent was crucial. There was no instance in which a son refused to be interviewed once his father had consented; and privacy was not an issue between the fathers and the sons. Once the father agreed that his son could be interviewed, he never insisted on being present.

On the whole the men were more curious than the women about the study: about who was sponsoring it, what its purposes were, and especially about the interviewers themselves. They asked the boys about their families, where they came from, how long they had lived in Israel, about the type of work they did, and about their religious convictions.[10] The interviewers always explained that although their families observed many of the traditional religious practices, they themselves did not. They did not observe the regimen of daily prayers or the dietary laws; and they were wearing a *kipa* out of respect for them.[11] In no instance did such a "confession" cause the loss of an interview.

The interviews in Mea Shearim were conducted over a period of six months. The more time that passed, the easier it became to gain acceptance by potential respondents. After a few months, the interviewers had become recognized and familiar figures in the community. Respondents in the later months often commented that they had heard about "an American professor who was making a research about us." Children in the streets stopped the interviewers and asked if they were going to their house. Later on, when we expanded the field work to include interviews with some of the influential figures in the community, we found that they had all been appraised of our presence and of what we were doing. One of them, Amram Blau, the leader of the Naturei Karta, acted as if he had been waiting for the interviewers to call upon him, having already heard some time ago from some of his followers about the American professor. Only rarely did prior publicity hurt the study. In a few instances when a family was approached, they said: "Yes, we have heard of this research, but our rabbi told us not to cooperate with you."

The situation in the Arab community was different. In part because the Arab community in Israel has been studied on other occasions on a variety of issues, we encountered fewer obstacles and less resistance. In addition, the Israeli Arab community does not have a tradition of cultural and moral superiority vis-à-vis the larger society. The Israeli Arabs do not believe that they have been "chosen" or that they are special. Indeed, the Israeli Arab community might better be characterized as suffering from a sense of collective inferiority or from a belief that they are underdogs and that theirs is the lesser or lower culture in the society. For all of these reasons, the Arab community was more accessible and more responsive to the survey.

The Arab interviewers were teachers who lived in Lod, Ramle, Haifa, and in nearby Arab towns. The supervisor was a schoolteacher who had had considerable experience working on surveys of Arab communities in Israel for the government, the Histadrut, and for private research agencies. He was also a man of some prominence in his own community. He was an elected member of the town council, and his family was known and well regarded in many Arab communities in the northern and central portions of Israel. He hired three of his male colleagues, all of whom could claim some experience moonlighting as interviewers. For the mothers and daughters, he hired two elementary schoolteachers, one of whom lived in Haifa, the other in Ramle; both had had experience working on surveys. The women were about the same age as the interviewers in Mea Shearim, which meant that they were about midway between the average age of the daughters and the mothers they were interviewing.

Since we had a sample frame that contained a list of the names of Arab families that were likely to have a son or daughter in the appropriate age bracket, we contacted each of those families initially by sending them a letter (in Arabic) describing the purpose of the survey and making a tentative appointment. If the time designated was not convenient, the family was asked to tear off the appropriate section of the letter, indicate another time on it, and return it in a prestamped envelope.

Most of the time, when the interviewer arrived at the home he was treated as a guest, which meant that he was invited to sit in a place of honor, and before the interview could proceed, he was served fruit, cigarettes, and coffee. There were practically no refusals among the Arab families contacted.[12] In the few instances in which there were, they were made by the sons, who demonstrated their unwillingness to participate by not being home at the appointed time and by making themselves unavailable at any other time. On the few occasions when this happened, the parents were embarrassed and apologetic.

Unlike the respondents in Mea Shearim, privacy was not a problem. Neither mothers nor fathers insisted on being present during the interview of a son or daughter; nor did any of them refuse to have their son and daughter interviewed. But also unlike Mea Shearim, the parents did not take it upon themselves to make their sons and daughters available. The interviewers initiated the contacts directly with the sons and daughters, and they informed the interviewers themselves, without parental intervention, whether they were willing to participate in the survey.

In sum, 100 fathers and 100 sons and 50 mothers and 50 daughters were interviewed in Mea Shearim; and 125 fathers and sons and 50 mothers and daughters were interviewed in the Arab communities. The parent interviews lasted about one hour and the son-daughter interviews about forty minutes.

3. Selective institutions in the two communities

This chapter provides background on three important institutions that, on the one hand, help sustain, insulate, and separate the ultra-Orthodox Jewish community and that, on the other hand, help provide a bridge by means of which the Arab community is able to establish closer contacts with the mainstream of Jewish Israeli society. The institutions are politics, education, and the mass media. We shall examine first the political institution as it serves the diverse needs of the ultra-Orthodox and the Arab communities.

Israel's political institutions

Israel's political structure most closely resembles that of Great Britain. It consists of executive, legislative, and judicial branches with a president (whose functions, like those of the British monarch, are mainly ceremonial and formal), a parliament, a cabinet, and a legal system. The parliament, or Knesset, consists of 120 members who are elected for four-year terms through a system of proportional representation. The cabinet is the executive branch, and it is headed by the prime minister, who may select members of his cabinet from within or outside of the Knesset.

Unlike the British system, however, there are no electoral constituencies in Israel. The whole of Israel forms one constituency. Each political party presents a list of up to 120 candidates, arranged in an order of priority determined by caucus. At the top of the list are the names of the party's active leaders, arranged by the party caucus. Each elector votes for a complete party list, and the number of party members elected is determined by the percentage of votes received by that list. If a party list secures, for example, 10 percent of the votes cast, it gains 12 out of the 120 seats, and the first 12 members on the party list are declared elected. If a member subsequently dies or resigns, the next person on that list is automatically seated. There are thus no by-elections as in Britain. In a small party, which never gets more than 5 seats, the rest of the 115 names on the party list are purely ornamental.

The cabinet or the government is responsible to the Knesset. A government cannot be formed without majority support in the Knesset and must resign when it fails to maintain the confidence of the Knesset.

As in the British system, the Israeli Supreme Court does not have the power of judicial review. It can invalidate administrative actions or interpretations of statutes that it regards as contrary to the rule of law, but it cannot declare a law passed by the Knesset unconstitutional.

The political parties that play a major role in contemporary Israeli life are to a great extent the same ones (perhaps with new names or new alignments) that were most important in the one or two decades prior to the establishment of the state. Since statehood the government has been in the hands of some type of Labor coalition. Prior to 1965, the name of the government party was Mapai; after 1965 Mapai and Ahdut Haavoda formed the Labor Alignment.[1] Both Mapai and Ahdut Haavoda are democratic-socialist in orientation, the former being somewhat to the right of the latter. Since 1965, the Labor Alignment, which subsequently included other smal'er leftist groups in its fold, such as Mapam, has formed the government.

The leading opposition party is Herut. It is to the right of the Labor Party on domestic/economic issues and in favor of a more aggressive and expansionist foreign policy. Its leader is Menachem Begin, who is the former commander of the Irgun (a dissident military force in Palestine that opposed the British and the Arabs) during the War of Independence.

Only once, during the First Knesset, did the four religious parties (Mizrachi, Labor Mizrachi, Agudat, and Labor Agudat) unite and support the Labor government. The unity disintegrated before the next election and the Agudat parties withdrew. In 1961, the labor branch of the Agudat Party rejoined the government coalition but did not reunite with the other (Mizrachi) religious parties.

In addition to these three major groupings Israel has two Communist parties; the older one, formed in the early 1920s, is Maqi, and the new one, formed in 1965 as a result of a split within Maqi, is Rakah. Rakah is the only independent party that has Arab leadership. There is also a Liberal Party, which at various times has joined Herut and at other times remained separate.

In all of the Knessets since 1949 (there have been seven) the Labor Alignment has usually maintained between 51 and 55 percent of the votes. Herut with its subsidiaries usually marshals about 25 percent, the religious parties about 15 percent. The Communists and other very small parties each manage to retain fewer than five seats.

Of all the third world countries that achieved independence following World War II, the government of Israel has been among the most stable. Israel has been free of the civil wars, the coups d'etat, the general strikes, or the military takeovers that have characterized other newly independent nations in Africa and Asia.

The political institutions and behavior of the ultra-Orthodox community

The social isolation and separateness that the ultra-Orthodox Jews manifest by their choice of residence, language, and style of dress is also apparent in their political behavior. By and large, the community is split into two camps. The much larger camp supports the Agudat Party, which is the most orthodox of the four religious parties, and the smaller group supports the Naturei Karta. Between 1949 and 1953 the Agudat Party joined in a coalition with the other religious parties and supported the Labor government. The head of the Agudat, Jacob Meir Levin, was awarded a seat in the first cabinet as the minister of social welfare. But in 1953, the Agudat left the coalition and has remained separate and independent ever since. Agudat represents about 45,000 voters and has four representatives in the current Knesset.

Within the government, the Agudat Party is the spokesman for the most orthodox elements in the society. Its position on domestic issues such as educational policy, military service for girls, observances of the Sabbath, and adherence to religious law on matters of marriage and divorce has consistently been the most orthodox. But within its own constituency of potential supporters, the views espoused by the Agudat Party are constantly under attack as being too moderate, and Agudat leaders have been accused of being too willing to compromise with secular interests. The group that directs the attack against the Agudat has been the Naturei Karta, which also draws its support from the residents of Mea Shearim and which was part of the Agudat movement until 1945.

The Naturei Karta is not a political party; it is a social movement, composed of perhaps three to five hundred families residing primarily in Mea Shearim. Naturei Karta means "Guardians of the City," and "guardians," as it is used in this context, means teachers and protectors of the Sacred Law, "without which Judaism would cease to exist." Until his death in 1974, the leader of the Naturei Karta in Jerusalem was Amram Blau.

The split between the Agudat and Naturei Karta is a relatively recent one. The Agudat movement was founded in 1912. Its support came mainly from the shtetl Jewry of Eastern Europe. In 1935 Agudat members from Poland and Germany began arriving in Palestine in relatively large numbers. The leaders of the Agudat during its European period were strongly opposed to the Zionist movement and to any movement that sought the establishment of a Jewish state. In 1935, however, the Agudat began to work with other forces in the Jewish community in Palestine for freer immigration policies to Palestine and for greater control within Palestine.

It was during this period that supporters of the Agudat movement who had been living in Palestine prior to the 1930s and who had maintained their resistance to Zionism and Jewish autonomy lost control of the Agudat Party and never regained it. Beginning with the late 1930s, the Agudat Party moved toward affiliation with the larger Zionist cause. Between 1940 and 1947, the Agudat cooperated with the national Jewish institutions in Palestine in their policies toward the British authorities. These activities were enhanced by the arrival of the leader of the Agudat Party in Poland, the Hasidic Rabbi of the Gur dynasty, and his son-in-law Jacob Meir Levin. It culminated in Agudat's joining with other Jewish groups in demanding that the United Nations vote for partition and establish a Jewish state in Palestine. In 1947 the Agudat Party was granted official recognition in the Provisional Council of State, and its leaders joined in signing the Declaration of Independence in May 1948.

During the period from the mid-1930s until the establishment of the state, elements within the Agudat Party strongly attacked Agudat for its cooperation with the Zionists. In 1945 this group, which was dominated by the older settlers within the ultra-Orthodox community in Palestine, formally severed its connection with the Agudat Party. According to Marmorstein (1969:90), it was in 1945 that a group of Jews in Jerusalem first came to be publicly identified by the name Naturei Karta. Their leaders were Aaron Katzenellenbogen and Amram Blau. That severance continues to the present time.

In contemporary politics, the Naturei Karta stands as a reminder to the Agudat Party, and to ultra-Orthodox Jewry as a whole, of the compromise that Agudat made with Zionism, which means with nationalism and secularism, and of its willingness to go along with the Zionist establishment. The Naturei Karta, for example, publicize the financial subsidies that Agudat receives from the government as a result of its compromise. Thus, although the Agudat Party claims that it maintains an independent school system, a basic goal of which is the perpetuation of ultra-Orthodoxy, the Naturei Karta points out that 85 percent of the Agudat school's budget comes from the government. Every time the government passes a law, or makes a ruling that is inimical to the interests of the ultra-Orthodox community, the Naturei Karta publicizes the fact that Agudat Party representatives sit in the Knesset, not mentioning, of course, that the Agudat representatives opposed the particular actions of the government and opposed them loudly and bitterly.

When former Prime Minister Levi Eshkol died in 1970, and some of the Agudat representatives in the Knesset attended his funeral, the Naturei Karta, on the day following the funeral, distributed leaflets throughout Mea Shearim calling attention, in a disparaging manner, to the presence of Agudat Party leaders at the funeral of a "non-observant Jew."

Since the establishment of the state in 1948, the Naturei Karta has been the only Jewish group that has remained outside the institutionalized political sphere in the name of religious orthodoxy. Its followers do not vote, do not carry identification cards, do not enroll their children in schools that receive any kind of governmental subsidy, and do not avail themselves of the judicial, medical, or other services supplied by the state. They are clearly "in" but not "of" the society. They perceive themselves as the "traditional Jewish conscience."

The particular issues about which Naturei Karta has been most outspoken in recent years have been the mass conversions in Vienna of Soviet citizens on their way to Israel, the practice of performing autopsies on Jewish patients in government and private hospitals, the calling of girls for military service or any kind of government "social" service in lieu of military service, the transgressions of the Sabbath by the Egged Bus Company, and performances of dramatic and symphonic works that are considered obscene because of their sexual connotations or because of their religious or political implications. The performance of a symphony or a concert that has Christian symbolism would be a case in point.

The Naturei Karta usually makes its objections known by public demonstrations, acts of civil disobedience, the distribution of pamphlets, and the placement of posters on the buildings in Mea Shearim. Yeshiva students at Naturei Karta institutions generally are the most visible participants in such activities, and they have engaged in physical confrontations with the police.

In the spring of 1971, after a series of demonstrations directed primarily against the Egged Bus Company that resulted in damage to several buses, the stoning of passengers, fracasses with the police, and the subsequent arrest of dozens of yeshiva students, the walls of buildings in Mea Shearim were covered with posters describing the prior evening's events in Jerusalem as the "Jewish Night of Crystals."[2] The Israeli police were referred to as the "Gestapo." Mea Shearim was described as the "Jewish section of Jerusalem." Posters stated that the Naturei Karta could not receive a fair and an impartial hearing in any Israeli court and that a special UN commission should be convened to hear the cases of the young men arrested by Israeli police.

In March 1975 the body of a man who died at one of the major hospitals in Jerusalem (Shaare Zedek) was snatched from the hospital by a group of yeshiva students. The *Jerusalem Post* carried the following account.

When the police arrived, after being summoned by the hospital administration, the students took the body out of the morgue through a side exit and took it to their yeshiva. The police were barred entrance to the yeshiva by a crowd of students.

Israel Sun photographer Mike De Castro reports that the body was returned after hospital director-general Prof. David Maeir explained to the yeshiva head that permission had been obtained from the necessary sources.

Shortly afterward, a group of nearly 100 members of the Committee for Human Sanctity stormed the hospital, smashing windows as they looked for the body. They were finally banished from the premises by club-swinging police. They refused to believe Prof. Maeir's statement that Rabbi Weiss approved the autopsy, and only after confirmation of this fact from the rabbi himself did they disperse and the autopsy proceed. (1975:3)

The Naturei Karta has followers outside of Israel. In sheer numbers, it has more supporters in London, Manchester, and New York City than it does in Jerusalem and B'nai Brak. Its most prominent leader, Joel Teitelbaum, the head of the Satmar Hasidic community, lives in

Williamsburg, Brooklyn. Until early in1974, the leader of the Naturei Karta in Mea Shearim was Amram Blau, a man in his middle seventies who has been photographed with yeshiva students at demonstrations against Sabbath transportation, at various cultural events in Jerusalem, and at rallies against mass conversions or autosies.

News of Naturei Karta's activities appeared in the American press (*Los Angeles Times* and *New York Post*) in 1975 with the following account of their pro-PLO (Palestine Liberation Organization) sympathies.

While Israel's attempts to negotiate with Egypt were dominating the headlines, a group of Orthodox Jews here was quietly opening its own lines of communication with the Palestine Liberation Organization.

The Watchers of the City (Naturei Karta, in Hebrew) share the PLO's opposition to Zionism, but for different reasons.

These deeply religious Jews (fanatics, their critics say) maintain that a state of Israel has no right to exist until the coming of the Messiah.

The Jews were sent by God into exile in punishment for sin, the Naturei Karta say, and until the Messiah comes, the Jews are bound by "divine oaths" to take no forcible action to regain the Holy Land.

They see Yasir Arafat, leader of the PLO, as their natural ally in their opposition to the present Jewish state.

PLO statements from Beirut last month indicated that should a Palestinian government-in-exile, be formed, certain anti-Zionist Jews would be included in it.

Following this, Naturei Karta publicly indicated a willingness to act as "consultants on Jewish affairs" under a government-in-exile but would not actually accept an official cabinet post in such a body.

Even the consultancy arrangement would be a spectacular victory for the PLO, because it would lend credibility to Arafat's expressed desire to form a "secular democratic state."

Official Israeli policy is predicated on the assumption that Arafat wants to destroy Israel and push the Jews into the sea.

The reaction of most Israelis to Naturei Karta's flirtation with Arafat was shock and anger. Questions were asked in Parliament about whether the Naturei Karta had not breached the law in communicating with the enemy.

However, because the organization is careful to conduct its contacts through its members in cities overseas there is no apparent grounds for prosecuting Naturei Karta members in Israel.

"Our offices abroad now are in the process of arranging consultations with the PLO in their respective countries," said Rabbi Moshe Hirsch, 40, from New York's Lower East Side, who is the group's official spokeman. (Drummond 1975:6)

It is important to remember, however, that even if the Agudat Party and the Naturei Karta were to combine forces, they would still represent only a tiny proportion of the Israeli public. Together or separately, they are unlikely to hold any kind of pivotal power in Israeli elections. But their presence is important, nevertheless, and they leave a significant mark on Israel's political life. Although the secular or the less observant Israelis do not share their views, many of them respect and favor retaining aspects and practices of public life that are consistent with the ultra-Orthodox perspective.

It is this position that allows the Agudat Party to remain in the government and that also allows the Naturei Karta to play the same role vis-à-vis the Agudat that the Agudat plays toward the more liberal religious parties such as the Mizrachi. Both elements push the groups closest to them toward adopting a stronger, and perhaps a more extreme, stand on more issues than they would if they did not know that there were forces behind them that would make capital of their failures. Thus in Mea Shearim the Agudat supporters must always be on the alert to ensure that the Naturei Karta has not found any issues on which they have been lax or remiss in adequately representing the ultra-Orthodox position.[3]

Looking ahead, there does not seem much likelihood that the position of either the Agudat Party or the Naturei Karta will change significantly or that either will experience a drastic expansion or decline in public support. The Agudat is hopeful that at least some small proportion of the Russian Jews, especially those who have emigrated from the Soviet state of Georgia, will support them. Naturei Karta will probably retain both its present size and disproportional visibility. Should there be peace between Israel and the Arab nations, the amount of domestic strife between the ultra-Orthodox Jews and the rest of the society could increase considerably. Should such conflict increase, the leaders of the Agudat Party might think it expedient to seek an alliance with the Naturei Karta in order to prevent it from becoming politically isolated. The Agudat Party might then return to a position close to its pre-1947 stance in order to expand its hegemony over the entire ultra-Orthodox community.

The political institutions and behavior of the Arab community

Since the establishment of the state a large majority (over 80 percent) of the Israeli Arab population has consistently voted in national elections. Most of the Arab vote has been in support of the "Arab lists" that have been under the aegis of the Mapai Party or, since 1965, under the banner of the Labor Alignment coalition.

In the election to the first Knesset in January 1949, 33,000 Arabs were eligible to vote in the newly formed state. Of those, 79.3 percent voted, compared with 86.9 percent of the Jews who were eligible to vote. Later data reveal that this election marked the low point in Arab voting. In every subsequent election to the next six Knessets, the proportion of Israeli Arabs who voted was as high or higher than the proportion of Jews.[4]

The voting behavior of those who voted in the first Knesset turned out to be predictive of Arab voting trends in every subsequent election. The distribution in 1949 was as presented in Table 3.1.

According to Landau (1969:76–7),[5] the Arab lists are not Arab political parties, but in fact ad hoc groups that are inactive between electoral campaigns. The candidates on those lists usually represent wealthy and influential Arab families from regions in Israel having large Arab populations. Landau quotes a young Israeli Arab nationalist's attitude toward the candidates on the Arab lists:

These are not our representatives. They ignore the interests of the Arab population. Together with the local Arab politicians, they are more dangerous to the State than to the Arab population itself because the Arab problem cannot be solved through a separate struggle, or a separate Jewish struggle, but only through a common struggle. They are opportunists and hence negative characters (1969:77).

Table 3.1. *Distribution of Arab votes in 1949 Knesset election by party*

Political party	Percent of Arab votes	
Mapai	9.6	61.3
Arab lists allied with Mapai	51.7	
Religious parties	0.6	
Herut	0.4	
Mapam	0.2	
Party of Oriental Jews	11.4	
General Zionists	3.6	
Maqi	22.2	
Others	0.2	
Total	100.0	

The proportion of Israeli Arabs who voted in all of the subsequent elections and the parties for which they voted are described in Tables 3.2 and 3.3.

The pattern shown in Tables 3.2 and 3.3 has been a fairly consistent one over the seven elections. The government party and its Arab lists retained a majority of the Arab voters over the twenty-year period. In those years in which it lost support — for example, from 1959 on — it was because parties to the left of it had gained in strength. In 1959 it was Mapam that gained in strength. Between the elections for the Second and Third Knesset, Mapam publicized its policy of Arab membership, and the gains in strength among the Arab electorate may be a reflection of that policy.

Until 1965, Maqi Communist Party was the only party that had included both Arab and Jewish members from 1948 onward.[5] The Communists began their political activities and recruitment among the Arabs under British rule. Although a majority of the party members were Jewish, by 1961 Arabs composed about one quarter of the party membership. Some of its leading spokesmen were also Arab: Tawfik Tubi and Emil Habibi, the party's representatives in the Knesset, and Emil Toma, one of the party's leading theoreticians. The major planks in the party's platform have been demands for equal rights for Arabs, the ceasing of land expropriation, improvements in education and employment opportunities, and other improvements in the Arab standard of living.

Table 3.2. *Percentage of Arabs who voted in the Knesset elections*

Knesset	Percent of Arabs who voted among those eligible	Percent of Jews who voted among those eligible
First Knesset (1949)	79.3	86.9
Second Knesset (1951)	85.5	—
Third Knesset (1955)	91.0	82.8
Fourth Knesset (1959)	88.9	81.6
Fifth Knesset (1961)	85.6	81.6
Sixth Knesset (1965)	87.8	83.0
Seventh Knesset (1969)	85.6	81.7

Source: Landau (1969:108—5); Central Bureau of Statistics (1970*b*).

Table 3.3. *Percentage of Arabs who voted in Knesset elections by year and party*

Political party	First 1949	Second 1951	Third 1955	Fourth 1959	Fifth 1961	Sixth 1965	Seventh 1969
Labor, Mapai, and Allied Arab	61.3	66.5	62.4	52.0	50.8	50.1[b]	56.9
Mapam	0.2	5.6	7.3	12.5	11.0	9.2	—[d]
Maqi	22.2	16.3	15.6	10.0	22.7	5.0	—
Rakah[c]	—	—	—	—	0.7	22.6	28.9
Others[a]	16.3	11.6	14.7	25.5	15.5	18.1	14.2
Total	100.0	100.0	100.0	100.0	100.0	100.0	100.0

[a]Other parties are the Religious parties, Herut, Ahdut-Haavoda, the Liberal Party, and the General Zionists.
[b]In 1965, Mapai is the same as the Alignment, and it includes Adhut-Haavoda. It lost some of its former supporters who organized Rafi, such as David Ben-Gurion and Moshe Dayan.
[c]In 1965, there was a split within the Communist Party and most of the Arabs affiliated themselves with Rakah.
[d]In the elections for the Seventh Knesset in 1969, Mapam joined the Labor Party.
Source: Landau (1969:108–55); Central Bureau of Statistics (1970*b*).

In 1961 Maqi increased its Arab support by more than 100 percent. It is during this period that the Arabs made their strongest demands for the abolition of military administration, the settlement of all land claims, and the suitable employment of young Arab intellectuals. The Maqi Party with its Arab spokesmen in the Knesset organized much of the Arab protest. By the summer of 1965 the split between most of the Jewish faction and the Arab faction within the Communist Party was complete and Rakah (the New Communist Party) was formed. All of the Arab members of Knesset (MKs) who had previously represented Maqi became spokesmen for Rakah, and Rakah became the only party in Israel with a majority of Arab members.

Landau estimates that in 1965–6 at least 70 percent of Rakah's members were Arabs. While both Maqi and Rakah are non-Zionist, Rakah attacks on the Jewish state are more pervasive. It supports all Arab "liberation movements" and is on friendly terms with most of the Arab states. Both Rakah and Maqi seek support from the Israeli Arab student population and young Arab intellectuals.

A further breakdown of the Arab vote from 1949 to 1969 by region shows that Arabs in urban centers supported the Communists (Maqi through 1961, and then Rakah) to a much greater extent than did the Arabs in the villages and the Bedouin tribes. For example, in 1961, 1965, and 1969 the votes for Rakah and the Arab lists were distributed as shown in Table 3.4.

In part because the government placed restrictions on Arab political activities and in part because there was a lack of leadership, an Arab nationalist movement on a large scale has not developed among Israeli Arabs. The one attempt at such an organization, Al-Ard, was founded in 1958. In 1964 it was banned by the Ministry of Defense. The Supreme Court supported the Defense Ministry's order stating that "the list" denied the existence of the state and wanted to cause its destruction. In his decision, the president of the court wrote, "No free regime would grant assistance and recognition to a movement that undermined its own existence." Al-Ard was a non-Communist nationalist organization whose appeal was greatest among the young Arab intellectuals. With its demise in 1964 and the formation of Rakah in the summer of 1965, no other Arab nationalist movement has emerged.

Along with the absence of a nationalist movement, except for Al-Ard, has been the absence of a Muslim religious political party. Given the close relationship between religion and politics in the other Arab states in the Middle East, the absence of such a political party among Israeli Arabs is worth noting. Perhaps the leading Muslims in Israel be-

Table 3.4. *Arab voting patterns: 1961, 1965, and 1969*

Location	Labor Alignment			Arab Lists			Maqi	Rakah	Rakah
	1961	1965	1969	1961	1965	1969	1961	1965	1969
Arab towns	4.6	3.4	5.6	36.9	34.9	38.9	45.0	42.0	45.9
Large Arab villages (i.e., 2,000 or more)	7.3	8.3	12.1	46.4	44.2	37.9	25.5	23.1	31.7
Smaller Arab villages	7.5	13.6	21.5	45.7	43.1	48.0	13.0	13.1	13.1
Bedouin tribes	18.4	12.0	24.2	54.2	49.9	51.5	2.7	4.5	5.1

Source: Landau (1969:108–55); Central Bureau of Statistics (1970*b*).

lieve that their interests are best taken care of under the Labor Alignment umbrella and prefer not to risk forming a separate political base
that might then be taken over by younger Arabs whose political lean-
ings would be more nationlist or leftist than could be supported by the
party in power.

Since 1949 there have been nineteen Arab representatives in the
seven Knessets. Most of them (ten) have been farmers. The others have
designated their occupations as follows: journalist and politician (three),
journalist (one), landowner (one), lawyer (one), farmer and lawyer
(one), architect (one), clerk (one). Except for the first election when
there were only three Arabs in the Knesset, two from the Arab lists and
one from Maqi, there have been either seven or eight Arabs elected to
each subsequent Knesset. Four or five were usually elected from lists
supported by Mapai or the Labor Alignment, and the other two or
three have come from Maqi (after 1965, Rakah) and Mapam. Their geographical base matches those areas in Israel in which most of the Arabs
live, the northern part known as the Galilee, the little triangle area in
the center of the country, the town of Nazareth, and the city of Haifa.
In the Knesset the Arab representatives usually concentrate on topics
that are of special interest to the Arab minority: demands for the relax-
ation of the military administration; pressures for raising the standard
of living of the Arab minority; requests for larger budgets for roads,
clinics, and schools; and efforts to make available better opportunities
for employment for young Arab intellectuals.

Educational institutions in Israel

With the founding of the state, a law was passed that provided for compulsory education for all children five to thirteen years old. The
Compulsory Education Law of 1949 left intact until 1953 the then-
existing organization of the educational system, which was linked to
the political parties. Between 1949 and 1953 the choices that parents
had concerning the types of elementary schools they wished their
children to attend were: (1) general (supported by the secular center
and right-wing parties); (2) labor (supported by the leading party,
Mapi); (3) Mizrachi (the National Religious Party); and (4) the Agudat
Israel (the ultra-Orthodox Religious Party). In addition a very small
minority (about 1 percent) sent their children to ultra-Orthodox
schools that received no government support.

In August 1953 the Knesset passed the State Education Law, which abolished the formal connection between educational tracks and political parties. The new law offered parents of children a choice between state education and religious state education schools. The aims of state education were based on

the values of Jewish culture and the achievements of science, on love of the homeland and loyalty to the State and the Jewish People, on practice in agricultural work and handicraft, on pioneer training, and on striving for a society built on freedom, equality, tolerance, mutual assistance, and love of mankind. (Kleinberger, 1969:123)

The state system also included separate schools for Arab children. The aims of religious state education were essentially the same, save that "its institutions are religious as to their way of life, curriculum, teachers and inspectors" (Kleinberger, 1969:124).

The 1953 law also authorized the minister of education and culture to prescribe conditions for the recognition of nonofficial institutions, impose upon them the obligatory basic program, supervise them, and assist them financially. The Agudat Party has taken advantage of this option and has maintained the autonomy of its independent school system while at the same time accepting state subsidies.

Thus, at the present time in Israel, there are three educational tracks. About 65 percent of the children attend the state schools; about 25 percent attend the religious state schools; and about 8 percent attend the school in the Agudat system. There continues to exist the completely independent system that is sponsored and directed by the Naturei Karta and some Hasidic groups. Those schools account for about 2 percent of the school population.

The next two sections describe in some detail the educational system as it operates within the ultra-Orthodox community of Mea Shearim and among the urban Arab population.

The educational institutions of the ultra-Orthodox community

In large measure the success of Mea Shearim as a community is attributable to the foresight and energy that the elders and leaders of the community devote to providing for and anticipating the social, physical, psychological, and economic needs of its members, especially the needs of its children. One of the topics that the parents in our survey were mostly likely to discuss after the formal interview had been completed was the importance of providing enough stimulation, activities, and satisfaction to retain the loyalty and devotion as well as the physical presence of their youth. Said more colloquially: The parents expressed concern about how they would be able to keep their youngsters "on the farm," after they had seen Paris or Vienna or Kansas City.

In one context or another, Jews have faced this problem since the destruction of the Second Temple and the loss of their sovereignty some 1900 years ago. Poll and Rubin in their studies of the ultra-Orthodox community in Williamsburg address this issue directly. Jews have been more successful in some parts of the world, and in some eras, than in others in retaining their identity as a community and in maintaining the loyalty and sympathy of their youth. The larger society's practice of forcing Jews into ghettos may have caused them in centuries past to retain their identity. Later, when ghetto walls were removed and travel restrictions lifted, many Jews in Europe, North Africa, Asia, as well as the United States, opted to remain in self-imposed ghetto communities, from which they had the freedom to move in and out and from which they could conduct business activities, but to which they could also return for social and psychological security and support.

As we stated earlier, for the ultra-Orthodox Jews in Jerusalem, Mea Shearim represents such a self-imposed ghetto. Indeed, the residents often refer to their neighborhood as the "Jewish section" of Jerusalem. For them, the larger society is as alien and unattractive as the larger Gentile culture was for the Jews who lived in the Diaspora in the nineteenth and twentieth centuries; the important distinction is, however, that the residents of Mea Shearim are not in any physical danger from the larger alien society. But, as we noted earlier, during periods of conflict with the representatives of the dominant culture, the residents of Mea Shearim have referred to the Israeli police as the "Gestapo" or as "Cossacks" and have referred to the attacks upon them as "pogroms." Nevertheless, most residents of the area do not feel that the hostility the larger society directs toward them places them or their community in any danger of being destroyed. But the analogy of how Jews in the Diaspora conducted themselves is a useful and a meaningful one for them; and the steps they take to retain their unity and the continuity of their community are not unlike the measures Jews of prior eras had taken in Eastern or Central Europe to preserve their identity.

This concern is manifest most prominently in the steps they have taken to control and direct the education of their children. Over 90 percent of the children in Mea Shearim attend schools that are under the supervision of the Agudat Party or that are independent of the state system or of any religious movement that is affiliated with the state. The schools in the latter category, which include yeshivas, and talmud torahs, for boys, and nursery, elementary, and secondary schools, and teachers' seminaries for girls, are generally under the direction of the Naturei Karta or a particular Hasidic sect such as Satmar. In maintaining this complex network of educational institutions that accept children from two years of age until adulthood (for the men there is no age limit), the ultra-Orthodox community is able to retain a large measure of authority over its youth. The Agudat schools, like those that are completely independent, are segregated by sex. Hebrew is the language of instruction in the Agudat school at least at the elementary level and for the girls at the secondary level.

According to the State Education Law, the Ministry of Education and Culture can impose upon the independent, nonofficial religious schools (which describes the status of the Agudat schools) a basic curriculum that is to comprise at least 75 percent of the total weekly lesson periods. The other 25 percent of the time may be spent as the system itself wishes. In the Agudat system it is usually devoted to traditional religious subjects, the Bible, the Talmud, and the liturgy.

Table 3.5 summarizes the differences among the curriculums of the three approved schools: the state schools, the religious state schools (comprising generally the National Religious Party or the Mizrachi perspective), and the Agudat schools.

There are Agudat schools throughout the country that serve girls of elementary school age. They have been in existence for more than forty years and are called the Beit Yakov schools. There are seven Beit Yakov elementary schools in Jerusalem. The one most easily accessible to Mea Shearim has 500 children ranging from first through eighth grades. The language of instruction is Hebrew. All of the teachers complete two years of training in Beit Yakov seminaries following their graduation from secondary schools.

In the main, the Agudat schools have the equipment, the furnishings, and the decorations that one associates with other elementary schools in the Israeli state system. Textbooks are available, and there are pictures and other appropriate decorations on the walls in the rooms and

Table 3.5. *Allocation of weekly lesson periods in selected grades of Hebrew primary schools*

Subject	State schools Fourth grade	Fifth grade	Religious state schools Fourth grade	Fifth grade	Agudat Israel schools Fourth grade	Fifth grade
Old Testament	5	5	6	5	7 (10)	7 (10)
Oral law			2	7	5 (−)	9 (−)
Prayers and religious laws	−	−	4	−	4 (3)	1 (3)
Hebrew language and literature	5	5	3	3	2 (3)	3 (4)
Heimatkunde and		2				2 (3)
geography	3		2	3	1 (2)	
Nature study	2					1 (2)
Arithmetic	4	4	3	3	3 (3)	3 (3)
Physical education	2	2	1	1	1 (1)	1 (1)
Art and music	2	3		2		1 (2)
Handicrafts	2	2–4	3	2–4	1 (2)	4 (2)
Agriculture	2			2	− (−)	
Social education	1	1	−	−	− (−)	− (−)
Total	26	26–28	26	26–28	24 (24)	32 (30)

	Seventh and eighth grades		
Old Testament	4	5	5 (9)
Oral law	1	7	10 (3)
Hebrew language and literature	3	3	3 (3)
Arithmetic and geometry	4	4	3 (3)
History	3		2 (2)
Geography	2	4	1 (1)
Natural science	2		1 (1)
Foreign language	4	4	2 (3)
Physical education	2	2	1 (1)
Art and music	2	1	1 (1)
Agriculture and handicrafts	2–4	2	3 (5)
Social education	1	−	− (−)
Total	30–32	32	32 (32)

Note: Figures in parentheses refer to girls' schools.
Source: Kleinberger, 1969:170.

in the hallways; there is also a yard in which the children are able to play during recess.

In the independent schools — that is, those not connected with the Agudat system — the language of instruction is Yiddish. Like the Arab youth, then, these ultra-Orthodox Jewish children receive an education that places them at a disadvantage vis-à-vis the larger society. For some of the ultra-Orthodox Jews, as well as the Arabs, Hebrew is a second language that they learn in later years in school or that they pick up on the street. For many, then, Hebrew is never a language with which they feel completely comfortable.

The largest and most important of the independent schools for girls is B'nat Jerusalem (Daughters of Jerusalem).[6] It was founded shortly after the establishment of the state by supporters of Naturei Karta with about 30 students. In 1971 it had over 1,200 students ranging from two through eighteen or nineteen years of age. Almost all of the teachers at B'nat Jerusalem are former graduates of the school. The language of instruction is Yiddish. Both the headmistress of the school, a woman in her seventies who has directed the school since its founding, and the members of the board of directors said that they emphasized the importance of tradition and of preparing the students to be "good Jewish wives and mothers." In the words of some of the respondents, the school prides itself in teaching its students "nothing that is new."

One member of the board stated the purpose of the school in these terms:

We want these children never to feel ashamed of their grandmothers. We want them to have the same *Weltanschauung* as that held by Jewish daughters one hundred years ago. We do not aim to prepare our pupils for higher or advanced education. There is no thought that the graduates of B'nat Jerusalem would seek entry into institutions of higher learning upon graduation from B'nat Jerusalem.

Intellectual stimulation in and of itself is not valued. The transmission of the Jewish tradition with special emphasis on the woman's role in that tradition is emphasized above anything else at B'nat Jerusalem.

The school has three main divisions: (1) a nursery and kindergarten division, which has children between two and a half and six years of age; (2) an elementary division, which includes grades one through eight; and (3) a seminar, which includes grades nine through eleven. The girls attend school for twenty-five hours a week, five hours a day, five days a week. Unlike the state schools, there is no school on Fridays, presumably because the teachers as well as the pupils need the time at home to prepare for the Sabbath.

The curriculm is divided such that 75 percent of the time is devoted to academic studies and 25 percent to sewing, embroidery, and knitting. The teachers emphasized the importance of teaching sewing and other handicraft courses. The clothes worn by the girls in this community help establish their identity. They are distinctively different from those worn by other Israeli girls, and they are difficult to come by in the ready-to-wear market. The girl who is not taught how to sew well enough to supply her own wardrobe needs might be tempted to look at the merchandise on display in the shops in the center of Jerusalem. One of the major purposes for teaching handicraft skills is to insulate the girls from such temptations.

The secular subjects include arithmetic and mathematics through elementary algebra and geometry, history, almost exclusively that of the Jewish people, and geography. The texts that the teachers use to prepare their lessons are those employed in the Agudat school system. But since the texts are in Hebrew, the teachers translate all of their materials into Yiddish and prepare lesson forms in Yiddish for the children to use. About ten hours a week are spent on secular subjects; the other fifteen hours are spent on religious subjects, including the Bible, prayers, ethics of the fathers, and Jewish laws, particularly those pertaining to ritual.

The teachers earn about one-third of the salary of teachers who are employed in the Agudat system. Each teacher negotiates her own salary with the director, who makes her decision on the basis of years of experience, the grade in school that the teacher is expected to teach, and the teacher's economic circumstances, that is, her marital status and if she is married, her husband's situation, and the size of her family.

Each student is expected to contribute something to the costs of running the school, but like the teacher's salary, each family negotiates the fee that it must pay.

Although the manifest function of the school is education, none of the people who are involved in making policy concerning the institution believes that the teaching of specific cognitive skills or the expanding of intellectual horizons is the major purpose of the school. Rather, its major purpose is believed to be the socializing of its pupils so that they are prepared to play the roles that will be appropriate to their future status as traditional Jewish wives and mothers. In other words, it is the teaching of a life style that will help assure continuity for the community.

The director stressed the strong ties that exist and that must exist between the school and the parents. The nature of the ties is such that it is the school's responsibility to reflect the parents' values and not establish itself as a source of conflict between parents and children. Should there be conflict between the parent and child, it is the school's policy to support the parents.

The same basic schism that exists between Naturei Karta and the Agudat schools for girls may also be found among the boys' schools at the elementary and secondary levels. Both the Agudat and the Naturei Karta movements have a network of talmud torahs and yeshivas that differ in their language of instruction, in the amount of time devoted to secular subjects, and in the image that is projected of the place that their community occupies in the larger society. Like the girls, the boys enter the school system at the age of two, but, unlike the girls, the boys begin their formal religious studies at the age of three, in the talmud torah. A talmud torah is the equivalent of an elementary school. It includes a secular curriculum in addition to religious studies. About 5,000 boys study in talmud torahs all over Israel.

The language of instruction in the non-Agudat schools is Yiddish. The Naturei Karta schools devote less time to secular studies, but the hours of instruction are longer than in the Agudat schools. In those talmud torahs in which the language of instruction is Yiddish, there are no texts and the teachers either prepare translations from Hebrew texts in geography and history and distribute mimeographed lesson plans or do without written materials.

The teachers in the independent schools are usually from the yeshivas. They are usually married men who find it difficult to maintain themselves and their families on the stipends they receive for studying at the yeshivas. The salaries usually paid to the talmud torah teachers are at least double those that the women teachers receive at B'nat Jerusalem or Beit Yakov, but less than male teachers receive in the Agudat system.

Upon graduation from the talmud torah, a boy may enter a yeshiva. The yeshivas are both secondary schools and colleges. There are almost 5,000 in the former category and 4,000 in the latter. In most yeshivas, all of the secular subjects are discontinued and the curriculum is devoted completely to sacred or religious studies.

The time spent in the yeshiva is much longer than the time spent in the talmud torah. Students usually remain in the yeshiva for the entire day, except for a break at lunch. Their study is less organized than in other schools. The students either study alone or with one other student who is his study partner for an extended period of time. Some yeshivas expect their students to return in the evening for additional study or prayers or for discussions with other students. The yeshiva has more of the characteristics of a total institution than of a secondary school even though most of the boys do not live on the premises.

Bentwich, in *Education in Israel,* describes the talmud torahs and yeshivas as follows:

The talmud Torahs . . . still follow the tradition of Jewish education . . . almost unchanged; the content of instruction mainly religious subjects — Bible, Talmud, etc. — with only a bare modicum of Hebrew and arithmetic; the language of instruction often Yiddish; the teachers in long black coats, even in summer . . . They are not under Government control and receive no grants, but are recognized *de facto* if not *de jure* as exempting boys and their parents from the provisions of the Compulsory Education Law . . . The Yeshivot . . . central aim . . . is common to all: the study of Torah . . . as it has been studied for hundreds of years, largely individually. You will . . . see 100–200–300 boys or young men, reading their page of Talmud [aloud and all at the same time!] each to himself or in small groups and swaying to and fro as they read. [There are instructors to be consulted, and some individual testing] . . . but there are no certificates, no diplomas, no degrees. [Y]et many Yeshivot including those that teach no general subjects — nothing but Talmud and Bible and Musar from morning till night — are full to capacity and with long waiting lists! (1968:108–10)

The boys who attend yeshivas are distinctive not only in the clothes they wear (most of them wear the dress of the Polish aristocracy of the eighteenth and nineteenth centuries) and in the language they speak (Yiddish), but in the important fact that they are exempt from military service if they opt to remain in the yeshiva during the years ordinarily set aside for military training.

The independent yeshivas are also centers of political activities. Yeshiva students form the core of the demonstrations against violations of the Sabbath, theater performances that are considered obscene, and shops that cater to sexual tastes. The yeshivas also supply the leadership and the premises where the strategies and the tactics for the demonstrations are devised. The yeshivas that are under the auspices of the Agudat Party also serve as centers from which the party recruits its functionaries and leaders.

The length of time a boy remains in the yeshiva depends upon his motivation and interest in pursuing religious studies and on his financial situation. If the boy wishes to dedicate his life to the pursuit of knowledge of sacred texts, he may spend the rest of his life in the yeshiva. After he marries and has a family, he and his family may be taken care of for life assuming that he is willing to live frugally and within the social and physical sphere of the yeshiva. Should the young man not show sufficient promise or ability as a student, then the monetary arrangements that the yeshiva may be willing to make for him would probably not be adequate for him to provide for his family's needs; then he would be forced to seek regular employment and continue his sacred studies on an avocational basis.

Funds to support the yeshivas come from Orthodox Jews all over the world. The Agudat Party has an international branch with offices located in major cities in the United States, Britain, Australia, South Africa, and other places where there are well-to-do Jewish communities who raise funds for all of the education, health, and welfare institutions that the Agudat Party maintains in Israel. The Naturei Karta also has an international network with a large following in London, Manchester, and New York City that helps maintain the schools and other institutions and the activities of the Naturei Karta in Israel. The institutions and services of the Agudat Party and of the Naturei Karta could not exist on the scale that they do without support from Orthodox Jewish centers in North America, Great Britain, Australia, and South Africa.

Arab education in Israel

At the elementary school level, segregated schools on the basis of ethnicity is the rule in Israel. At the secondary school level, Arab youth who live in urban centers may attend schools in which the majority of students are Jewish and in which the language of instruction is Hebrew.

Only a small percentage of all Arab youth attend secondary schools of any type. In 1960 about 14 percent attended. Kleinberger has reported that in 1963–4 there were a total of 257 Arab and Druze youth enrolled in Jewish secondary schools (mainly in vocational and agricultural schools); in 1966–7, the number rose to 356. In 1966 for every 1,000 Arab adolescents aged 14–17, 228 were enrolled in secondary schools, compared with 620 for every 1,000 Jews of corresponding age (Kleinberger, 1969:197). At the college or university level the proportion was 10 out of 1,000 Arab youths. In 1970 there were 250 Arab students out of a student body of 15,000 at Hebrew University. At Haifa University, the proportion was higher, 350 Arab students out of a student body of 4,400 (Rabinowitz, 1972:47).

But the *number* of Arab students is only one aspect of the complicated problem of educating Arab youth in Israel. As Kleinberger commented in 1969:

[T] he most difficult problem concerning the education of the non-Jewish minority is still without a satisfactory solution. What are its aims? Even its practical goals, in economic respect, are beset by an inherent contradiction. On the one hand, the Ministry of Education is making considerable efforts to increase the number of Arabs who complete a secondary school and acquire a university degree. On the other hand, for those who possess a secondary or higher education there are very few adequate openings outside teaching.

The Arab sector itself has no industry and few social and administrative services of its own which can offer white-collar jobs to Arab graduates of secondary schools or universities. In the Jewish sector, social and cultural distance as well as alleged security reasons (which not infrequently are unfounded) and suspicion of the Arab's loyalty and reliability prevent their employment in any substantial number. In consequence, not a few of the educated young Arabs remain unemployed or are forced to accept employment in manual labor. (1969:320)

In the same vein, in 1962 the vice mayor of Nazareth, Abdul Aziz Z'uaba, wrote

There are today some 2000 youths who have completed their secondary schooling and have a good knowledge of both Hebrew and Arabic. They are seething with discontent in the feeling that they are deprived of full equality and barred from their rightful place in Israeli society . . . These young people have been educated at Israeli schools. They were four or five year old children when the state was established and may be categorized as "Israeli born." Yet they are generally refused acceptance to civil service posts or to clerical positions in other public institutions. Only about two percent of the Civil Service are Arabs. The discrimination practiced by the government as employer has set the tone for public institutions as well as private companies and banks. (1962:59-63)

The lack of suitable employment opportunities is an important aspect of the problem. It contributes to the special bitterness and animosity that educated Arabs in Israel have toward the state. An indication that the problem has not gotten better appears in a report of a survey that was commissioned by the prime minister's office and released in 1973. The main conclusion of that study, which was conducted by the Shiloah

Institute of Middle Eastern and African Studies, was that "Israel is facing an urgent problem in the form of Arab college graduates who cannot get the jobs they want."

The results were reported in the *Jerusalem Post*:

The survey also tried to measure satisfaction with work. Most dissatisfied were social workers, while on the whole, doctors and lawyers were pleased with their jobs. More than half of those interviewed said they wanted some other job.

Dissatisfaction centred principally on the difficulty in getting ahead or earning more money in what was essentially a Jewish society. Of secondary importance was the degree of responsibility they were given or the interest which the work itself aroused.

The Prime Minister's Adviser on Arab Affairs, Shmuel Toledano, said Tuesday that the Government is making "vigorous efforts" to secure more jobs for Arab high school and college graduates. He said that a circular had been sent to all Government services and public institutions instructing them to engage Arabs for vacant posts. (Weiss, 1973:4)

Another serious aspect of the education problem is the values and aims of the educational system and the intrinsic contradictions between those values and aims and the status of the Arab minority in Israel. In its broadest sense, an educational system socializes its youth to identify with its culture, to be loyal to its symbols, to value its institutions, and to obey its rules. In Israel, these goals apply not only to the state per se as a political entity but to the "Jewish people," historically and demographically. The loyalty that is sought is not only to a state, but to a people with a particular historical, religious, and cultural *Weltanschauung.* The educational system is supposed to train children to identify with that *Weltanschauung,* which includes Israel as a state, and the Jews as a people.

How do such goals apply to Arab youth? Can the educational system make "Israelis out of Arab children and still have them retain their Arab-Muslim (or Christian) identity? In part, the Israeli answer to this dilemma is to maintain separate educational systems — one for Jews and one for Arabs. But such an arrangement really only begs the questions or delays facing the problem. One must still resolve the issue of what is taught in the Arab schools and how much emphasis is placed on areas such as history, literature, social studies, and science.

According to Eisenstadt and Peres, Israeli educational authorities claim that the aims of Arab education are to achieve a synthesis of the central values of the Jewish majority culture and of those held by the minority. The crucial issue in their minds is: How can we encourage loyalty to Israel among Israeli Arabs without demanding a negation of Arab aspirations, on the one hand, and without permitting the development of hostile Arab nationalism, on the other? With this aim in mind, the criterion for evaluating the curriculum in Arab schools was translated by Eisenstadt and Peres as follows: "To what extent does it help the young Israeli of Arab origin to see his path clearly and to mold his own identity in a way which maintains a reasonable balance between his Arab nationalism and his loyalty to the state in which he lives?" (1965:63)

In their study of the Arab educational system in Israel, Eisenstadt and Peres compared the number of hours Jewish students in secondary schools and Arab students in secondary schools spend studying Jewish history, Arab history, and world history. The results are reproduced in Table 3.6.

As shown in Table 3.6, the Arab students' curriculum contains half as much Jewish history as the Jewish students' curriculum, but there is no comparable carry-over of Arab history for Jewish students. The Jewish curriculum pretty much ignores Arab history and concentrates on Jewish and world history.

Another major difference between the Arab and Jewish curriculum is the greater number of hours the Arab students devote to literature and language. This difference is described in Table 3.7.

Table 3.6. *Hours devoted to studying Jewish, Arab, and general history in Jewish and Arab secondary schools in Israel as a percentage of total hours spent on history*

History	Humanities curriculum		Science curriculum	
	Arab secondary school	Jewish secondary school	Arab secondary school	Jewish secondary school
Jewish history	20.2	38.8	20.6	40.9
Arabic history	19.1	1.4	19.5	2.1
World history	60.7	59.8	59.9	57.0
Total hours of history in each faculty	416.0	416.0	384.0	484.0

Source: Eisenstadt, 1965:69.

Table 3.7. *Number of hours spent on literature and language in Jewish and Arab*
secondary schools in Israel, by type of curriculum

	Humanities curriculum			Science curriculum		
	Jewish school	Arab school		Jewish school	Arab school	
	Hebrew	Hebrew	Arabic	Hebrew	Hebrew	Arabic
Literature	512	340	420	352	340	420
Language	256	172	404	256	172	404
Total	768	512	824	608	512	824

Source: Eisenstadt, 1965:40.

Not only do Arab students spend considerably more time studying Arabic literature than Jewish students spend on Hebrew literature, but, in addition, the Arab students spend many hours on Hebrew literature as well. On the matter of religious studies, here again Arab students are required to study Jewish religious texts, as well as the Koran. But Jewish students are not exposed to the texts of religions other than their own.

It appears thus that the Israeli educational system exposes Arab students to their own heritage, to the Jewish Israeli heritage, and to world history; but practically no efforts are made to expose the Jewish Israeli to the Arab heritage. Certainly if Israel is to succeed in synthesizing the minority culture with the majority, the majority must be educated to understand the contribution of the minority tradition. From where is that understanding to come, if not from the educational system? As Eisenstadt and Peres have observed, "the official curriculum demanded that Arab youth should learn first and foremost the principles of a national culture in which they were not allowed to participate." Atallah Mansour, the Arab correspondent for *Ha-Aretz*, the leading morning newspaper in Israel, wrote:

The stories of youths who have come into contact with Jewish young people in school and at places of work often lead to the dismal conclusion that this section of the Arab population is more hostile to the Jewish society than any other Arab element. The young Arab hates the Jewish society because it regards him as strange and different and rejects him because of envy for his Jewish counterpart who outdoes him culturally and intellectually. (1962:59-63)

The problem of the appropriate curriculum represents one large portion within the maze of problems that is associated with the education of Arab students in Israel. Another aspect of the problem is the availability and quality of Arab teachers. In 1947—8, during the fighting between the Israeli and the Jordanian, Egyptian, and Syrian forces, most of the Arab community that lived in Palestine migrated to the neighboring Arab countries. Many of them were following the instructions of Arab leaders to leave "temporarily" and then return in the wake of an Arab victory over the Jewish forces. After that victory they would then assume the leadership of a newly established, independent Arab state instead of the Jewish state imposed upon them by the United Nations. Others left out of fear of how they would be treated in a Jewish society.

Whatever the reasons for the exodus, those who left represented most of the educated, middle-class, Arab community who had provided much of the economic, political, and cultural leadership of the Palestinian Arabs. Those who remained had little to lose at the hands of a Jewish government. The mass exodus thus left a hiatus in the number of trained Arab teachers necessary to direct and teach in the Arab schools in Israel. Those who were most qualified to teach, or those families who were likely to have children who would receive training as teachers, left in 1948. The problem was acute immediately following the establishment of the state. It is still large and serious twenty-nine years later. Besides the lack of teachers, there is a scarcity of texts and a need for better physical facilities. At the present time, there is one Arab teachers' college in Israel and no other Arab institutions of higher learning. The problem of educating Israeli Arab youth at all levels remains a serious, and as yet still a largely unresolved, problem.

The mass media in Israel

There are at least ten languages spoken by various communities in Israel. Aside from Hebrew, Arabic, and English, Russian, German, Yiddish, and French have the largest constituencies. The daily and weekly newspapers cater reasonably well to the diverse needs. Newspapers are published every day in at least three languages, Hebrew, English, and Arabic, and weeklies are published in a variety of other languages that include Russian, Hungarian, German, Roumanian, French, Spanish, and Yiddish. The two leading Hebrew language newspapers, *Ha-Aretz* (a morning paper) and *Ma'ariv* (an evening paper) are independent; that is, they are not the organ or mouthpiece of a political party. The *Jerusalem Post* appears daily in English and is also independent of any of the political parties. In addition, each of the major parties — Labor, Herut, Mizrachi, Agudat, and the Communists — has either a direct and formal connection with a newspaper or an informal tie, but one that nevertheless results in that paper consistently representing the views of the particular party.

Both radio and television are under the authority of the state. Television is relatively new, having been introduced in 1968, and at the present time Israel has only one channel. Hebrew is the major language employed; but every evening about a quarter of its programming is devoted to topics of interest to the Arab community, and the programs (news, human interest, children's affairs) are conducted in Arabic. The Israeli radio caters to about as many language communities as does the press. Programs throughout the day and night may be heard in German, Russian, Yiddish, English, Spanish, as well as Hebrew and Arabic.

The ultra-Orthodox media

More than any other community in Israel, the residents of Mea Shearim must generate their own sources of information and commentary about the larger society, about Jews in other parts of the world, about international affairs generally, and about many other important topics, because most of the ultra-Orthodox leaders have insisted that their followers not expose themselves to the typical fare available from either the domestic or foreign press and electronic mass media.

It is important to reiterate that the objections that ultra-Orthodox Jews have to television particularly, but to radio as well, are not the usual objections of a sacred community to instruments of modern technology. The ultra-Orthodox Jews, in contrast, for example, to the Amish or the Hutterite communities in Europe and North America, have not animosity, moral or otherwise, to the spread and use of technology or modernization per se. They use washing machines, refrigerators, automobiles, and so on, to the extent that they can afford to purchase such machines.

The ban on exposure to Israeli television and radio is based on objections to the content of the programs; it is the belief of the Naturei Karta and of many Agudat leaders that the materials presented are immoral, distasteful, and obscene or, at best, of a frivolous and trivial nature. Thus many of the respondents in our study answered the question about their exposure to the mass media by saying that they listened to the news and to certain suitable programs, such as "Hasidic Melodies," or Yiddish-language programs.

The nature of the Naturei Karta's ban is even more pervasive. It asks for total abstinence because the use of such facilities implies the granting of legitimacy to the state, since television and radio in Israel are run by the government. Availing one's self of any of the government's services is another opportunity for the state to co-opt the people. Abstinence, then, has a political-symbolic value for the Naturei Karta, over and above the feelings its members have about the content of the programs.

During the period in which our survey was conducted, a woman in Mea Shearim whose husband had been killed in the Six Day War used part of her pension money to buy a television set. When the neighbors heard of the woman's intention (they saw a television aerial on the roof of her building and the set being moved into the apartment), they stoned her. She was hurt badly enough to require hospitalization. After that incident, the walls in several buildings in Mea Shearim had the following posters attached to them:

NOTICE OF REPRISAL

Whereas — [name of person] refuses to heed the warning of the Beit Din [religious court] to remove a television set from his home [which is under the Beit Ya'acov synagogue], therefore, he falls under the strict excommunication, decreed by the Beit Din at the time against the introduction of television in Jewish homes. And his sentence is expounded in the Yoreh Deab, Chapter 334. [The Yoreh Deab is a section of the Jewish Law that lays down that no one should eat, drink or sit within four cubics of an excommunicant.] Nor is he to be counted in a minyan until he repents and removes this defiling and disgusting object from his home.

And we have signed our names below, on the strength of the Torah: The Beit Din of Jerusalem, The Holy City.

Newspapers and other press media do not enjoy a higher status among the ultra-Orthodox community. The Agudat position appears to be that the content of the Israeli press is not fit for the eyes of Orthodox Jews because it deals too much with sex, entertainment, sports, and other immoral and decadent matters. Also, on political grounds, the press has not shown sufficient sympathy to the ultra-Orthodox position on almost all important issues.

Since 1950 the Agudat Party has been able to publish its own daily

newspaper, *Hamodia.* It is printed in Hebrew and is sold mainly by sub-
scription. The editor estimates that it is mailed to about 1,000 homes
throughout Israel, with the heaviest concentration in Jerusalem. *Hamodia* is linked to the network of news-wire services that serves all of
Israel, but according to the editor at least 30 percent of the materials
obtained from the wire services are not fit to print. *Hamodia* also scru-
tinizes all advertisements and accepts only those that are consistent
with the moral and political tone of the paper. It carries neither advertisements nor information about movies, theaters, sporting events, or
other forms of entertainment such as concerts, dance recitals, or art
exhibits. The editor emphasizes that the newspaper is not necessarily
against all these activities, but that it perceives its role as providing a
counterculture and that therefore it goes out of its way to disassociate
itself from the mainstream of Israeli newspapers.

In recent years *Hamodia* has made the following topics its major
issues: a change in the law so that no women should be drafted into
the armed services, especially girls who do not wish to serve; exemption
of yeshiva students from military service; subsidization of all educational systems by the state; a change in policy so that autopsies would
not be performed on the basis of medical advice alone, but with the
consent of the rabbi; and the imposition of greater restrictions on
Sabbath work permits.

In addition to *Hamodia,* Agudat has a weekly newspaper, *Modiin,*
which focuses on religious issues and on Agudat interests in the Knesset.
It also publishes bulletins aimed at its youth and women.[7]

The Naturei Karta relies primarily on leaflets, posters, and signs on
the buildings in Mea Shearim for communicating with its followers,
sympathizers, and potential adherents. It also occasionally publishes a
magazine in Hebrew entitled *The Wall.* A Yiddish weekly, *The Light,*
which has a translated version in English for American and British
audiences, also reflects the Naturei Karta's position, although the
editors do not acknowledge Naturei Karta's endorsement or control.
The *Light* has an audience of about 8,000 in Israel and over 10,000
readers abroad. The size of its audience indicates that it has appeal
among the ultra-Orthodox community as a whole, not only among followers of Naturei Karta. The *Light's* major political themes have been
attacks on the mass conversions of non-Jews who emigrated from the
Soviet Union, the practice of autopsy, inappropriate styles of dress
among women, and desecrations of the observance of the Sabbath.

To conclude, for a community as small as the ultra-Orthodox in Israel (the 50,000 or so Agudat supporters and the 1,000–2,000 Naturei Karta followers), the number, diversity, and frequency of its publications are impressive. But remember that these publications are not meant as a supplement to the fare that is already available in the society as a whole. They are an exclusive substitute for the rest of the Israeli mass media. In that context, then, their number may not appear as impressive.

The Arabic media

Literacy has been a significant limitation, at least insofar as the older members of the Arab community are concerned, on how much and how effective their exposure to the press in Israel can be. But since the arrival of television in 1968, Israeli Arabs have had a choice of watching at least ninety minutes of Israeli programming in Arabic every evening or of receiving programs from Jordan, Egypt, Lebanon, and Syria. The Israeli-originated programs carry news, human-interest stories, children's programs, and variety shows. Israeli radio stations also play Arabic music, broadcast news, and other types of programs throughout the day. And, again, Arabs in most parts of Israel can receive programs that originate in the neighboring Arab countries. The survey data show that a large proportion of the Arab community avails itself of the television and radio opportunities that originate both in Israel and in the neighboring Arab states.

From 1948 until the end of 1967, the Histadrut (the National Labor Organization) financed the publication of the only daily newspaper that appeared in Arabic, *Al-Yom* (The Day). The editor in chief and most of the editorial and reporting staff of *Al-Yom* were Jews. The more militant Arabs considered it a mouthpiece for the government and not a source of, or a reflection of, Arab opinion. According to Landau, one of the major functions that the newspaper served was to emphasize the positive achievements of Arab policies of the Israeli government. It also served to blunt the edge of the opposition press, as well as of the broadcasts from the Arab states. In 1966 the readership of *Al-Yom* was estimated at about 4,000 on weekdays and about 5,000 for the weekend edition. That period represented the peak of its support. It usually sold between 2,000 and 3,000 copies.

Al-Yom, however, ceased publication following the Six Day War in 1967. Since then, another daily, in Arabic, has been founded under quasi-governmental auspices. *Al-Anba* (The News) is the heir to *Al-Yom*. "It is more varied than *Al-Yom* was, it has more Arab journalists on its staff and it opens its pages to political discussion between different currents of opinion" (Stendel, 1973:180). Like its predecessor, it faces its stiffest competition from the various Rakah publications.

Al-Ittihad (Unity), a weekly published in Arabic by Rakah is probably the most influential newspaper among urban Israeli Arabs. Its circulation is estimated at between 4,000 and 6,000. Its articles reflect Rakah policy completely, and thus it is consistently opposed to the government's stance on all major issues concerning Israeli domestic policy, Arab policy, and foreign policy. Since its break with Rakah, Maqi has also begun publishing a fortnightly in Arabic called *Sawt-Al-sha'b* (The Voice of the People), but it does not have the circulation nor does it appear to have the influence of *Al-Ittihad.*

Mapam also publishes a weekly in Arabic, *Al-Mirsad* (The Observation Post). It has appeared since 1951 and it continues to reflect a somewhat independent view even after Mapam's affiliation with the Labor Alignment. Unlike *Al-Yom,* many members of the editorial staff of *Al-Mirsad* are Arabs and editorial policy is largely in Arab hands. Since Mapam's alignment with the government, *Al-Mirsad* has modified its position on broader policy issues that affect the Arab states. But it has continued consistently to advocate the abolition of all military administration for Israeli Arabs and greater assistance to local Arab affairs.

In addition to the daily *Al-Yom,* and the Mapam- and Rakah-sponsored weeklies, there are several monthly magazines in Arabic, one of which is *Al-Rabita* (The Bond), an organ of the Greek Catholics, It has appeared since 1952 and is published in Nazareth. Another Arabic monthly that is independent of any political party is *Al-Musawwar.* It has appeared since 1955. According to Landau, it is a combination of sensationalism on matters of sex and personal exposure, and political extremism. Rakah also publishes a monthly, *Al-Gad* (Tomorrow), that is aimed primarily at youth, and another, *Al-Jadid* (The New), which contains mainly translations of Communist works into Arabic.

In summary, the Arabic press in Israel is divided into two major categories: those publications that describe and defend the government policies vis-a-vis the Israeli Arabs and those that attack and criticise those policies. Radio and television, because they are run by the Ministry of Communications, do not contain pro and con aspects, nor are the Arabic programs as political in content as are the newspapers and magazines.

PART TWO

This part reports the results of the surveys conducted among the ultra-Orthodox and the urban Arab populations. Chapters 4 and 5 provide social profiles of the two communities. The profiles characterize the status that each family member occupies and the roles that the parents and children perform within the family, the community, and the larger society.

Chapters 6 and 7 analyze each of the families by comparing the sex role expectations within each generation. Chapters 8 and 9 represent the heart of the study. They assess the extent to which there is convergence between the expectations that the fathers and mothers have for their sons and daughters and those that the children have about themselves. They focus on those issues and topics about which there is consensus and on those over which there is strain and tension between fathers and sons, and mothers and daughters, within each of the communities. Chapter 10 contains a prognosis about the likelihood for, and the extent of, changes in the life styles and in the priorities of these communities. It considers issues such as whether the next generation of ultra-Orthodox Jews and Israeli Arabs is likely to change its religious commitments, the division of labor between men and women, marriage arrangements, the size of the families, educational and occupational aspirations and achievements, and involvement in the political and social activities of the larger society.

4. A profile of the ultra-Orthodox community in Mea Shearim

The fathers

Among the fathers in our survey 61 percent were born in Israel. The others came from Poland, Russia, and other countries in Eastern Europe. More than 60 percent arrived before 1948. Half of them came before their countries were overrun by the Nazis in World War II. Most of the others arrived after they survived the concentration camps, as the displaced persons' camps were emptied of their occupants. Once having arrived in Israel, they tended to remain in one place: Over 50 percent reported that they have lived in the same neighborhood for at least thirty years.

Most of the fathers are between forty-five and sixty years old; the mean age is fifty-three. The average number of children is 6.1, but the range is from 1 child to 12 children per family. The mean number of children reported by the mothers in our sample is 6.7. Both these numbers are considerably higher than the 2.3 that is the average for the rest of Jewish Israeli society.

Ultra-Orthodox Jewish men probably spend a greater proportion of their adult lives learning or studying than do other people anywhere else in the world. Forty-five percent reported that they attended school for more than sixteen years. An additional 13 percent claimed that they attended school for between thirteen and sixteen years. Over 90 percent of all of the fathers' schooling was in religious schools — yeshivas. The fathers also reported that their fathers' education was similar to their own, save that half of them thought that their fathers had had a better religious education than them. But the amount of education their wives received is markedly different. According to the men, 67 percent of their wives attended school (religious schools) for eight years or less. Except for 5 percent of the wives who are teachers, all of the others are housewives.

The work that most of the men do for a living is related directly to the schooling they have received. Of the 76 percent who claimed that they are employed, 55 percent said that they work in a synagogue or religious school.[1] They are rabbis and teachers in the yeshivas or talmud torahs, or they have some clerical or administrative post in the religious schools. The others are entrepreneurs in small shops in the neighborhood (13 percent), clerks in government agencies (11 percent), skilled craftsmen (15 percent), and laborers (6 percent). The stability that marked their residential pattern is also apparent in their work life. More than three quarters of those who work said that they have worked in the same job for at least ten years. Forty-three percent of the fathers of these men also worked at jobs that were related to their religious training and interests.

The picture that emerged of the occupations of the husbands from the women who were interviewed matched those drawn from the male respondents. For example, 49 percent of the women said that their husbands worked at jobs in religious institutions.

Asking people how much money they earn is always a sensitive topic; and it is often one that respondents refuse to answer. Among the Orthodox Jews in Mea Shearim it is a particularly sensitive and private matter. Many of them are the recipients of "gifts" from organizations abroad that arrive on a regular basis and for which they probably do not pay taxes. Some receive "help" from the yeshiva in which they study and work; others receive help from individuals who admire their piety. The fact that 55 percent of the men and 54 percent of the women (when asked about their husbands' income) refused to answer one or more of the questions about their sources and amounts of income illustrates how sensitive the topic is. With such a high proportion refusing to answer, reporting the responses of those who did may not be of much significance; however, almost all of those who refused held jobs that are connected to religious institutions. Practically all of those who are employed as clerks, businessmen, and laborers answered the income question. Forty-four percent said they earned less than 500 I.L. (Israeli pounds) per month; 53 percent said they earned between 500 and 1,000 I.L.; and 7 percent said they earned more than 1,000 I.L. per month.[2]

Questions about whether the respondent was receiving financial "help" on a regular basis also met with resistance. Sixty-five percent said that they did not receive help on a regular basis, that they supported their families through their own labors. Eighteen percent refused to answer the question. In this context we believe that a refusal to answer may be considered as an indication that the person or persons interviewed are receiving some type of regular financial aid. The other 17 percent acknowledged receiving help, and almost all of them said that the major source was the yeshiva in which they studied and prayed.

Language usage among the ultra-Orthodox men illustrates perhaps as dramatically as any single index can, the extent of their separation from the larger society. Only 3 percent of the fathers reported that they speak Hebrew primarily or exclusively in their homes. Eighty percent said they speak *only* Yiddish at home; and the remaining 17 percent speak Hebrew, and Russian or Polish, along with Yiddish. Even at work, only 20 percent reported that they use Hebrew primarily or exclusively; an additional 21 percent speak Hebrew and Yiddish; 49 percent use Yiddish exclusively. This latter group are the men who spend their days in the yeshivas and synagogues. But 85 percent use Hebrew on some occasions: when shopping, for business, or in their contacts with government agencies.

The fathers' responses to the items that asked about the newspapers they read is another indication of their distance from and their antagonism to the main currents of the society. Fifty-five percent do not read any newspaper. Failure to do so on the part of these respondents should not be attributed to a lack of literacy, nor to the absence of newspapers in the language of their preference, since newspapers in Yiddish, Polish, Russian, and Hungarian are readily available. The choice not to read any newspaper is a voluntary one, made for ideological reasons. Obtaining information about and demonstrating interest in public affairs through the medium of the press might signify involvement, commitment, and support for the state. Among the supporters of the Naturei Karta such attitudes do not exist; refusal or failure to read a newspaper thus becomes an act of protest.

Two-thirds of those who do read a newspaper, read only *Hamodia,* the official organ of the Agudat Party. It is printed in Hebrew and carries some international and domestic news. But it is given over largely to accounts of the Agudat Party's activities in Israel and in the United States, Britain, and South Africa. Exposure to other mass media is even more limited: Forty-five percent said they listen to the radio, but only to the news for, at most, an hour a day. Two percent watch television. No one attends the cinema.[3]

Still another powerful index of the estrangement that the ultra-Orthodox men have from the mainstream of Israeli society is represented by the fact that 39 percent do not vote. They claim that they have never voted or in any other way participated in an Israeli election. This percentage is especially significant in light of the fact that 90 percent of those eligible to vote in Israel do exercise their right of franchise, at least in national elections. Among those who claim they do vote, 42 percent said that they vote for the Agudat Party exclusively. The remaining 19 percent refused to say which party they support.

The consistent pattern that emerges from these responses about language, exposure to the mass media, and voting is that a sizable minority of the men in the ultra-Orthodox community live apart from the mainstream of Israeli society. In their manner of dress, in the way they spend their time, in the language they speak, in their isolation from the mass media, in their unwillingness to participate in national elections, they maintain a life style that has strong similarities to the lives their fathers and grandfathers led in the ghettos of the more enlightened countries of Central and Eastern Europe in the nineteenth century.

The army is another important institution in which the ultra-Orthodox community does not participate. Since the establishment of the state, one of the sources of pride, and one of the indicators of egalitarianism in Israeli society, has been the observance of a national policy whereby all Jewish citizens between the ages of seventeen and forty-five serve in the army. Only one Jewish group has been officially exempted from that practice: men who are students at the yeshivas and who claim that service in the army is objectionable to them on religious grounds. From time to time the Israeli Parliament debates the rightness and wrongness of that exemption. Whenever those debates occur, they are always characterized by extraordinary bitterness. Military service is one of the most important signs of loyalty to and membership in the society. The fact that most Orthodox young men do choose to fulfill their military obligations may be viewed as a sign of its importance.

When the fathers were asked whether they had ever served in the Israeli army, two-thirds of them said they had not. Among those who had, 7 percent served in the reserve, 6 percent had been members of the Haganah (the Israeli defense force before the establishment of the state), and the remaining 20 percent served in the army during the War of Independence in 1948. When the fathers were asked what they thought their sons would do, or had done, about their military service, and how they felt about their sons' plans, 21 percent said that they expected their sons to serve and that they approved of that decision. Two percent thought their sons would serve, but they opposed the idea. Ten percent said they would leave it up to their sons, that they recognized that both study in the yeshiva and obligations to the army were legitimate and important. The remaining 67 percent did not expect their sons to serve in the army and did not feel that they should serve because it is inappropriate to their life style, and an unnecessary compromise with secularism.

The ultra-Orthodox Jews do not have the same objections to military service that traditional Christian pacifist groups such as the Quakers and the Jehovah's Witnesses have. In their day-to-day living, and in their encounters with the police, for example, the ultra-Orthodox Jews do not espouse the principle of "turn the other cheek." They have been known to respond violently to decrees, rules, and behaviors that they have found objectionable and inimicable to their way of life. As discussed in the earlier chapters, leaders of the Naturei Karta have organized demonstrations and have urged their followers to take to the streets as a means of expressing their disdain for some official ruling. For supporters of the Naturei Karta, the shunning of military service should be perceived as another aspect of their general boycott of the state and of government service. For others within the ultra-Orthodox community, it is part of their belief in the superiority of their way of life and their belief that anyone can serve in the army; but only the special and the chosen can and should dedicate their lives to the study of Sacred Laws.

The respondents' beliefs in the superiority of their culture, their life style, and their religious observances are also illustrated by their reactions to how children in their community are reared as compared with other children in the rest of the society. The fathers were asked to compare the education that their children receive and the education that the other children in the rest of the society receive; the quality of the relationship between parents and children in their community and the parent-child relationship in the larger Israeli society; the relationship between the sexes in their community and in the rest of the society; the emphasis that is placed on ritual and religious observances in both communities; and the ways that boys and girls are allowed to dress in both communities. The percentages shown in Table 4.1 summarize the fathers' responses to these items.

These responses illustrate the sharp distinction that the ultra-Orthodox make between the positive attributes of their own community and the negative inferior values that are considered prevalent in the larger society.

Another illustration, given in Table 4.2, of the low opinion these people hold of the larger society are the responses given by the fathers to a series of items which asked for their judgments about how people in the larger society spend their nonworking time, the attention they give to religious observances, and the relations that exist between men and women. The fathers' disapproval of these practices is clear and unequivocal.

Table 4.1. *Jewish fathers' opinions about behaviors and beliefs in their own community versus the larger society (percentages)*

	Within "our" community	The rest of society
How parents rear their children		
Approve	35	6
Disapprove — children not respectful enough	24	46
Disapprove — parents do not exercise enough authority over children	20	28
Disapprove — other reasons	17	5
No opinion	4	15
Education children receive		
Approve	94	7
Disapprove	5	89
No opinion	1	4
Style of dress and general appearance		
Approve	96	3
Disapprove	4	97
No opinion	—	—
Relations between the sexes		
Approve	99	2
Disapprove	—	96
No opinion	1	2
Ritual and religious observances		
Approve	96	3
Disapprove	3	94
No opinion	1	3

Table 4.2. *Jewish fathers' opinions about behaviors in the larger society* *(percentages)*

How people spend time	
Approve	1
Disapprove (spend too much time on frivolous activities)	80
No opinion	19
Attention given to religious observances	
Approve	3
Disapprove (too little emphasis is placed on such matters)	87
No opinion	10
Relations between the sexes	
Approve	4
Disapprove (too loose, women are too free)	47
Disapprove (not traditional)	37
No opinion	12

So much for the fathers' views about the larger society and the ties that they maintain with that society. Now we examine their relationships within the ultra-Orthodox community and the manner in which they spend their days. In response to questions about whether they belonged to any organizations, 38 percent said that they were members of at least one. The others claimed no affiliations with any organized groups, save for their yeshiva. Those who were affiliated named philanthropic and political groups that are associated with the Agudat Party, by way of loan funds and religious-education committees.

When we asked them to rank those activities in which they spent most of their time when they were not at work, 94 percent ranked prayer or religious study either first or second (81 percent ranked it first). The only activity that competed with religious study and prayers was spending time with their families. None of them said they attended concerts, sporting events, union meetings, or that they sat in cafés or other places of entertainment.

A final question was asked of the fathers: "If you had a chance to live your life over again, what aspects of it would you live the same, and what aspects would you live differently?" Eight percent said that such matters are predetermined and that it made no sense to even consider them. For the others, 32 percent said they would live their lives essentially as they had. Forty-four percent said the only change they would like to make is to have more time for religious study and prayer. The remaining 16 percent talked about better financial and economic circumstances, but within the basic structure of a life devoted to religious study.

The mothers

It should come as no surprise that the mothers' profile bears a close resemblance to the fathers'. Sixty-two percent of the women were born in Israel; the others had come from countries in Eastern Europe. Like the men, half of them had arrived before World War II, the others having come between 1945 and 1950. Also like the men, they tended to remain in the same neighborhood in which they had been born or to which they had moved upon their arrival in Israel. Sixty percent of the mothers reported that they have lived in the same neighborhood for at least fifteen years.

When the women were asked how arrangements for their marriage had been made, 60 percent said that the services of a professional matchmaker had been used; 24 percent relied on their parents and/or other relatives, without the intervention of a matchmaker; and 16 percent said that they and their spouse had chosen each other, without the intervention of parents or a professional matchmaker. Fifty percent said that no money had been exchanged as part of the marital arrangements. The other half described various financial patterns, the most common of which was that both the bride's and the groom's parents gave money directly to the newly married couple so that they could furnish their own apartment.

The mothers' mean age is forty-seven. The average number of children is 6.7, with family size ranging from 1 child to 15 children. When the mothers talked about having children or about their daughters having children, they often commented proudly that they "did not fool around," by which they meant they did not do anything to prevent pregnancies. They often pointed out that they believed in the directive set forth in the Torah: " . . . be fruitful and multiply." In fact, Jewish tradition imposes limitations on a couple's childbearing opportunities. The period during the month when the woman is "unclean" and therefore unapproachable by her husband may extend for many days, and the woman can exercise discretion as to its exact length. After her menstrual period, she remains unclean until she goes to the mikvah (ritual bath). Thus a woman who wishes to prevent or delay her next pregnancy may postpone going to the mikvah until she has reached another "safe period."

The first major difference between the mothers' and fathers' profiles occurs in the matter of education. Seventy-four percent of the women said they had attended school for eight years or less. But like the men, for however long they were in school, all except 12 percent attended a religious school. The education that the women reported about their husbands was similar to that reported by the male respondents: Twenty-four percent said that their husbands had had more than 16 years of schooling.

Ninety percent of the women are housewives. Seventy-four percent said they had worked outside their homes before marriage, doing sewing and embroidery, or as teachers, usually in nursery schools or kinder-gartens. Seventy-two percent said that their husbands were employed; the other 28 percent described their husbands as being lifetime students in the yeshiva. Among those employed, 49 percent were reported as having jobs in religious institutions.

Fifty-four percent of the women could not, or would not, tell us how much money their husband earned. In more than half of the cases the women said that they did not know. Among those who mentioned a specific sum, 33 percent said less than 500 I.L. a month, and the others between 500 and 1,000 I.L. per month. But 48 percent of the women also said that their husband's job was not the major source of financial support for their family. Charities supported by religious organizations provided the major source of supplementary funding; the government helped in about one-sixth of the cases. Adult children and other relatives were mentioned by only 4 percent of the respondents.

The women's language usage differed somewhat from that of the men's in that more of them said they spoke Hebrew regularly, and in their homes, and 36 percent said that they spoke Yiddish exclusively (in contrast to 3 percent and 80 percent, among the men). The rest spoke a combination of Hebrew and Yiddish or Yiddish and another European language and Hebrew. More of the women knew Arabic than did the men, and 12 percent reported using it when they were doing their shopping.

Mea Shearim is located almost on the border of what had been the Jordanian part of Jerusalem prior to June 1967. The section of what is today called East Jerusalem bordering on Mea Shearim is a major marketing and shopping area where prices are generally lower than they are in West Jerusalem. Many of the women also said they felt more comfortable shopping in East Jerusalem because there is a greater opportunity to bargain and because the clothes worn by the Arab women are more decent than those to which they would have to expose themselves and their children in the Jewish parts of Jerusalem.

The women's responses to the items about their contacts with the mass media suggest that they are less separated and insulated from the mainstream of Israeli society than are the men. Seventy-five percent of the women (in contrast to 45 percent of the men) read a newspaper regularly. One-third of them (in contrast to two-thirds of the men) read only the paper that is the official organ of the Agudat Party; the others read secular newspapers in Hebrew, Arabic, Yiddish, or some European language. Two-thirds listen to the radio, and most of them listen to all kinds of programs; music and stories, as well as news broadcasts. The women's responses concerning television watching were similar to those of the men: Only 16 percent said that they watch television (6 percent have their own sets), and none reported going to the cinema.[4] But when the women were asked why they did not watch television or did not listen to the radio, only a small fraction said that their religious beliefs forbade them to do so or that it was against the Sacred Law. Their answers were more likely to refer to tastes and interests, or they would say that they had no time for such frivolity. The men, on the other hand, almost always explained their behavior by calling upon a religious edict.

More of the women than the men also said they vote in the national elections: 74 percent of the women in contrast to 61 percent of the men. Like the men, almost all of them vote for the Agudat candidates.

The distinctions made by the men about how children are reared, the education they receive, their religious practices, and so on, in their own community and in the larger society, are shared by the women. The women's responses to the items shown in Table 4.3 indicate that they also consider their way of life much superior to that of the rest of Israeli society.

The women's negative evaluation of the larger society, as shown in Table 4.4, is also apparent in their responses about adult behavior.

Table 4.3. *Jewish mothers' opinions about behaviors and beliefs in their own Community versus the larger society (percentages)*

	Within "our" community	The rest of society
How parents rear their children		
Approve	85	8
Disapprove – children not respectful enough	4	34
Disapprove – parents do not exercise enough authority	–	10
Disapprove – other	6	28
No opinion	5	20
Education children receive		
Approve	84	12
Disapprove	10	78
No opinion	6	10
Style of dress and general appearance		
Approve	84	12
Disapprove	14	84
No opinion	2	4
Relations between the sexes		
Approve	94	6
Disapprove	2	90
No opinion	4	4
Ritual and religious observances		
Approve	94	6
Disapprove	2	78
No opinion	4	16

Even less then the men, the women are not joiners of organizations or clubs. Only 18 percent said they belonged to any formal association, and within this small cluster the organizations to which they belonged were some combination of educational, religious, and philanthropic societies. It should be noted that most of these women have at least four or five young children at home and are responsible for all of the work in their homes.

In response to the last item, about what aspects of their lives they would like to live in the same manner and what aspects they would like to live differently, 58 percent said they would choose to live their lives

Table 4.4. *Jewish mothers' opinions about behaviors in the larger society (percentages)*

How people spend time	
Approve	4
Disapprove (spend too much time on frivolous activities)	72
No opinion	24
Attention given to religious observances	
Approve	16
Disapprove (too little emphasis is placed on such matters)	78
No opinion	6
Relations between the sexes	
Approve	2
Disapprove (too loose, women are too free)	42
Disapprove (not traditional)	34
No opinion	22

essentially as they had. Ten percent said that an individual has no say about such matters because each person's life is predetermined. Among the remaining third who said they would like to make some changes, almost all of them talked about having more comfort in their lives, and not having to work as hard. They enumerated the improvements in their life that a washing machine, a better heating system, and a good refrigerator could make. None of the women mentioned needing more time for prayer and study.

The sons

All of the children in the study share the characteristic that they are sabras; that is, they are native-born Israelis. And all of them have been born since the establishment of the state in 1948. None of them, therefore, has experienced directly the ghetto life of Eastern Europe that was so influential in shaping the personalities of their parents and of most of the other adults in Mea Shearim. Almost 80 percent of the boys have lived in the same neighborhood since their birth. When they were asked where they expected to live after they were married, 72 percent said in the same neighborhood that they are now living. The others did not know where they would be living.

The boys range in age from sixteen to twenty-one; about half of them are twenty years old. All but 8 percent are still in school, and all of them attend a yeshiva. When asked how much longer they planned to remain at the yeshiva, 33 percent answered "all my life"; 12 percent said "at least until after I am married." The others said at least four more years or several more years (35 percent) or said they did not know how much longer.

Forty percent said that they could not answer a question that asked what kind of work they expected to do when, or if, they were no longer in school. Among those for whom the question was relevant, all but 10 percent said that they expected to work in a yeshiva or reside there as a student-scholar. Half of those who could answer the question also said that the choice of what they would do in the future was theirs; the other half said it was mostly or completely their father's choice. Only 10 percent anticipated that they would have any difficulty realizing their plans; and 75 percent had no idea about what their earnings might be.

Like their fathers, 82 percent of the sons said that they speak Yiddish exclusively in their homes. Only 6 percent speak Hebrew exclusively; the others rely on a combination of Hebrew and Yiddish, or Yiddish and a European language. In the Yeshiva, 66 percent use Yiddish exclusively; 9 percent use Hebrew exclusively; and the others use both. When shopping or doing business with the government 58 percent rely on Hebrew. Sixteen percent said they have friends with whom they speak only Hebrew. Thus, like their fathers, but less than their mothers, almost all of the sons use Yiddish as their first language, even though all of them were born into a society many of whose members scorn Yiddish as the language of the Diaspora and of the ghetto.

Only 26 percent acknowledged reading a newspaper regularly; and among them, about half read only *Hamodia* (the Agudat paper). Seventy-five percent do not listen to the radio (two-thirds of whom explained that such activity was forbidden); and those who do listen emphasized that they listen only to the news for about an hour a day. Three percent said they watch television; no one attends the cinema.[5] Thus a large majority of the boys have even less contact with the mass media than their fathers.

Additional evidence of the young boys' desire to remain apart is made apparent in their responses to two other items: (1) whether they have voted, or expect to vote, in the national elections and (2), most crucial of all, whether they plan to serve in the army. Fifty-six percent said they had never voted and did not plan to vote.[6] They explained that they had not voted and will not vote because they do not recognize the legitimacy of the state. Among those who have voted or who plan to vote, all but 14 percent support the Agudat Party.

Eighty-two percent of the boys do not plan to serve in the army; 5 percent have not yet decided. The remaining 13 percent plan to serve in the next year or two upon completion of their twelfth year in the yeshiva. When asked how they felt about serving or not serving in the army, 70 percent said, in effect: " . . . study in the Yeshiva is more important than serving in the army"; "the army is not a suitable place for religious boys." A small proportion asked: "Why should one serve in the army of a country the legitimacy of which one does not recognize?"

In addition to studying at the yeshiva, for between ten and twelve hours a day, how else do the boys spend their time? For two-thirds of them, prayers and discussion about various portions of the Talmud were ranked first. Spending time with their families was ranked second, and talking and walking with their friends was ranked third.

Except for a small minority (about 5 or 6 percent), the boys' friends come from the same community, from the same types of families, and from the same yeshivas. Some come from B'nai Brak (a suburb of Tel Aviv) and Safed (a city in the north), and they are in Jerusalem because they wish, or their fathers wish them, to study with a famous Talmudic scholar in a particular yeshiva that is located in Jerusalem.

Twenty-three percent of the boys were engaged to be married. Their brides (in three quarters of the cases) were selected with the help of a professional matchmaker. The parents selected the future brides of the others. Among those who are not engaged, all but 8 percent said they anticipated that their parents, with or without the intervention of a professional matchmaker, would make all of the arrangements. Fifty-six percent of the boys expect to live in their own apartments in Mea Shearim after they are married.

The topic that aroused the greatest embarrassment concerned the prospect of their becoming fathers. The boys blushed, fidgeted, and many insisted that the interviewer skip to another topic. Forty-six percent refused to say how many children they would like to have after they were married; and 29 percent said "as many as God allows my wife to have." Of the 25 percent who were willing to cite a figure, the smallest number was three, the largest, twelve. None of them said that they did not want to have children.

We asked about the kinds of interests they might have as adults, and whether they planned to involve themselves in the affairs of their community, through either social, political, educational, charitable or any other kinds of activities. Two-thirds of the boys said they did not, either because they planned to devote their lives to the study of sacred books and that was more important and more worthwhile than any other form of endeavor, or because a job would probably take up all their time and they had no interest in community affairs or services. Among the remaining third, religious and charitable activities were named most often.

The image that emerges from this profile is that of young men who are preparing to live the types of lives they see their fathers living and that they presume their grandfathers lived. It is a life devoted largely to religious study, in the main unencumbered by the need to find a wife, support a family, participate in civic activities, and serve in the army. More details about how closely the fathers and sons resemble each other in terms of their life styles, the roles they are expected to perform, and the responsibilities they are expected to assume may be found in Chapter 8.

The daughters

Like the boys, all of the girls were native-born Israelis. Eighty-four percent had lived in the same neighborhood for at least the past ten years. Their modal age was between eighteen and nineteen, and the range was from fifteen to twenty-one. Unlike the boys, only 57 percent of the girls were still attending school at the time of the survey. Of those who were no longer in school about 25 percent had attended for fourteen years. They had attended a teachers' seminary for two years following completion of secondary school. Most of the others had completed between ten and eleven years of schooling. All of them had attended a religious school. They stopped going to school because they either had completed their course, were needed to help at home, or were no longer interested in attending. Half of them, however, said they would like to go back to school to study nursing, handicrafts, or for college preparation.

Ten percent of those who were still in school attended a nonreligious school; most of the others were students at the Agudat school. About 12 percent attended religious schools supported by the Naturei Karta or Hasidic groups that share that perspective. Most of those still in school were in the eleventh and twelfth grades and expected to attend for one or two more years.

All of the girls expect to work outside the home when they finish school and before they marry. Two-thirds plan to be teachers. The others want to be nurses, medical technicians, or embroiderers. They say that their choice of occupation is their own. Practically all of the girls who are no longer in school are working outside their homes as teachers (40 percent), handicrafters (20 percent), nurses and medical technicians (10 percent), or with children (15 percent). None earns more than 500 I.L. a month.

What emerges most clearly from these responses are the large differences in responses of boys and girls to questions about schooling and jobs. Most of the boys are preparing themselves for a lifetime of study and contemplation. They plan to spend their days in the yeshiva, studying, praying, and discussing, in much the same way that they have been doing since childhood. Some will become teachers, some rabbis; and a few will leave the yeshiva and open a small shop, or work as a clerk in the post office, but not until they are older or after they are married and have a family. Most of the girls, on the other hand, expect to make some financial contribution to their parents' household before they marry. Their schooling is directed at some objective, usually a teacher's certificate or at least completion of the course of study in which they are enrolled. They do not perceive their formal education as an endless experience or one that continues until an external event intervenes such as marriage or the birth of the first child.

The girls' language usage is also different from the boys'. At home 45 percent speak Hebrew exclusively, and only 31 percent use Yiddish exclusively. The rest use a combination of both. A few also speak another European language. Outside their homes, 30 percent use another European language in addition to Yiddish and Hebrew.

Seventy-one percent of the girls read newspapers on a regular basis, and 67 percent listen to the radio every day. More than half read the secular press in Hebrew and listen to all types of programs on the radio. Among those who said they do not listen to the radio, less than 20 percent gave some kind of religious prohibition as the reason. Only 8 percent watch television, and no one attends the cinema.

Many more of the girls than the boys also expect to vote in the national elections. A large majority will vote for the Agudat Party; and 12 percent will not vote because they do not recognize the legitimacy of the state.

Responses to the items concerning language usage, contact with the mass media, and voting patterns revealed differences in the orientation of the boys and girls just as the ones about occupation and education had. The girls appear more interested in, more positive about, and more in contact with the larger society than do the boys.

The girls' friendship patterns followed those of the boys in that the large majority of them have as their friends girls who are attending or who have attended the same school they did and are from the same type of family and religious orientation. The school tie is even more important than the neighborhood for determining friendship.

In most instances the parents who refused permission for the daughters' interview did so because they had had an opportunity to look over the questionnaire, and they felt that the items dealing with marriage and children were too provocative and inappropriate. A few mothers said they would be willing to allow the interview if they could respond to those items in place of their daughters. Presumably, they would have had their daughter leave the room when that part of the interview was taking place. It was our experience however that only a few of the girls were embarrassed and resisted discussing these topics. The questions about the number of children they were likely to have, for example, seemed to be much less embarrassing for the girls than for the boys.

Fourteen percent of the girls were engaged, and all but two of them are engaged to yeshiva students who had been selected for them by their parents and professional matchmakers. The two girls whose prospective bridegrooms were businessmen had made their own choice. All but 11 percent of the girls who were not engaged said that they expected to have their husbands selected for them by their parents or a professional matchmaker. Forty percent indicated that they expected that their consent to the match would be solicited before any final arrangements were made.

Unlike the boys, almost all of the girls expected that their family, or more commonly both their and the groom's family, would provide money for the couple so that they would be able to buy their own apartment and furnish it. All of the girls expressed approval and satisfaction with the manner in which they expected their marriages to be arranged.

When they were asked about the number of children they would like to have, 14 percent refused to answer the question and expressed embarrassment and annoyance about the topic. But 57 percent said unequivocally, "as many as I can," "as many as my husband wants," or "as many as God gives me." None said fewer than three; most said five or six. Most of them had no preference between boys and girls; and they suggested that even the asking of such a question showed a lack of reverence on the part of the interviewer. Most of those who answered said they would like to have the same number of boys and girls.

With this discussion, we have completed the first phase of our examination of the four family roles that we plan to characterize within the ultra-Orthodox community of Mea Shearim: that of the father, the mother, the adolescent son, and the adolescent daughter. The next time we discuss these roles, it will be in order to illustrate the differences that sex imposes upon each of the generations.

5. A profile of the urban Arab community in Israel

This chapter parallels the previous one in that it provides a profile of the parental and male and female adolescent roles in the Arab family. We begin with the fathers.

The fathers

All but 5 percent of the fathers were born in Palestine prior to 1948. Eighty-five percent have lived in the same neighborhood practically all of their lives. The age range is from thirty-six to seventy, the average age being 52. The mean number of children is 5.8, ranging from 1 child to 15 children per family.

Seventy-five percent of the fathers have an eighth-grade education or less. Fifteen percent have no formal schooling. All but 9 percent have attended a religious school. Over 80 percent are currently employed full time. The ones who are not working are either retired or unable to find work. Among those in the labor force, 80 percent work as skilled and unskilled laborers. Their employers for the most part are private businessmen (52 percent) and municipal or national government agencies (32 percent). They represent a remarkably stable labor force, over 80 percent having worked at the same job for more than twelve years.

When the occupations of the fathers of these men are compared with their own jobs (see Table 5.1), we find that only 3 percent of the sons are represented in the occupational categories in which their fathers were most likely to be found. According to the sons, 32 percent of their fathers were farmers, and 14 percent were merchants or businessmen.

Unlike the ultra-Orthodox respondents, questions about income did not elicit any more hostility or resistance among the Arab respondents than did questions about any other topic. All of the fathers who were in the labor force answered the income questions. The distribution revealed by their responses is shown as follows.[1]

Less than 500 I.L. per month	25%
Between 500 and 700 I.L. per month	32%
Between 700 and 1,000 I.L. per month	42%

Half of the respondents also acknowledged that they received financial assistance from the government.

All of their wives, save 2 percent, are housewives. Only 12 percent of their wives had received more than an eighth-grade education, and 42 percent had had no schooling at all.

Arabic is the language spoken at home by all except 4 percent of the fathers, who speak Hebrew and English as well. At work, 25 percent use Arabic exclusively; the others use only Hebrew, or Hebrew and Arabic. Twenty-nine percent said they sometimes speak English with friends or when dealing with tourists.

Two-thirds of the fathers do not read a newspaper. For some the explanation is simple: They are illiterate or have had such limited schooling as to make it difficult for them to do so. Those who can read, read both the Arabic and Hebrew press. Practically everyone listens to the radio. One-third of the respondents said they listen only to programs in Arabic; the others listen to all types of programs in Hebrew and Arabic for several hours a day. Seventy percent own their own television sets. But unlike their radio-listening habits, most of the respondents watch programs in Arabic exclusively. They have a choice of programs that originate in Jordan, Egypt, Syria, and Lebanon as well as programs in Arabic that are produced in Israel. About half of the respondents owned

Table 5.1. *Occupations of Arab fathers and their fathers*

Category	Respondents' occupation (%)	Fathers' occupation (%)
Farmer	0.8	32.3
Professional	5.6	—
Merchant and businessman	2.4	13.7
White collar and salesman	7.2	11.3
Skilled laborer	32.3	18.6
Unskilled laborer	33.1	16.9
Other/retired/don't know	18.6	7.2

sets before Israel instituted its own television programming, which means that prior to 1968 they had relied solely on programs produced outside of Israel.

According to public statements that were made prior to the inauguration of television in Israel, one of the major factors that motivated the development of television in Israel was the political and educational value it was expected to have among the Arab community. We noted earlier that of the five hours of daily evening programming that are available in Israel, at least one and one-half hours are devoted to Arabic.

Only 3 percent of the fathers claimed that they do not vote in Israeli elections; another 22 percent refused to reveal the party they usually support. Practically all of the others said that they vote for the Labor Alignment. Rakah, the New Communist Party and the only political party that has Arab leadership, was supported by 3 percent of the respondents who were willing to acknowledge the party they supported. But even assuming that a large majority of those who refused to say which party they support voted for Rakah, the Labor Alignment Party would still have about 70 percent of the fathers' votes.[2]

About 20 percent of the fathers served in at least one army at some time in their lives. For most of them, it was the British army during World War II. About the same proportion (20 percent) think that their sons ought to serve in the Israeli army. The others believe that it would be inappropriate and undesirable for an Arab to serve in an army whose major function is fighting other Arabs.

When they were asked how they spend their nonworking time and whether they were members of any organizations, their responses indicated that the most popular activity was sitting with their friends, talking and playing cards in coffeehouses, or staying at home with their families. Thirty-eight percent belong to at least one organization. The organization named most often was the Histadrut, the National Labor Union. But no one claimed to be an active participant.

The fathers were asked to evaluate aspects of the parent-child relationship within their own community and within the larger Israeli community, which of course means the Jewish society. As the percentages in Table 5.2 indicate, most of the fathers approve of parent-child relations in both their own and the Jewish Israeli community. But note that when there is a big difference in the responses between the two communities, in response, for example, to the item on how parents rear their children and the education children receive, the fathers are more approving of behavior in the larger society than they are in their own community.

Their judgments about adult behavior in the larger society, shown in Table 5.3, also indicate a positive evaluation, especially in the realm of religious observances.[3]

The responses to the final item in which the fathers were asked what aspects of their life they would live the same and what aspects they

Table 5.2. *Arab fathers' opinions about behaviors and beliefs in their own community versus the larger society (percentages)*

	Within own community	The rest of society
How parents rear their children		
Approve	66	81
Disapprove — children not respectful enough	16	11
Disapprove — parents do not exercise enough authority over children	11	3
Disapprove — other	5	3
No opinion	2	2
Education children receive		
Approve	62	94
Disapprove	38	3
No opinion	—	3
Style of dress and general appearance		
Approve	58	53
Disapprove	41	46
No opinion	1	2
Relations between the sexes		
Approve	62	70
Disapprove	37	28
No opinion	1	2
Ritual and religious observances		
Approve	76	75
Disapprove	23	20
No opinion	1	5

would live differently if they had a chance to live their life over again, showed that 85 percent would make important changes in their lives. The basic change most of them would make would be to improve their standard of living by learning a skilled trade and by obtaining a better-paying job. The other aspect of their lives most of them wanted to change was the size of their families. If they could live their lives over again, 21 percent said they would have fewer children. None of the fathers mentioned that he would move from Israel to an Arab country, nor that he wished he had moved in 1948.

The mothers

The Arab women, like the men, were all born in Palestine. Ninety percent of them have lived in the same neighborhood for at least fifteen years, and 50 percent have lived in the same neighborhood since their birth. The mothers' average age is forty-two. The average number of children per family is six, with family size ranging from one child to thirteen children.

Almost twice as many women (29 percent) as men (15 percent) have had no formal schooling; and only 12 percent have completed more

Table 5.3. *Arab fathers' opinions about behaviors in the larger society (percentages)*

How people spend their time	
Approve	69
Disapprove (spend too much time in frivolous activities, spend too much time with friends)	27
No opinion	4
Attention given to religious observances	
Approve	85
Disapprove (too little emphasis)	13
No opinion	2
Relations between the sexes	
Approve	58
Disapprove (too loose, immoral)	32
Disapprove (not traditional)	9
No opinion	1

than eight years of school. Most of those who attended school went to religious schools.

Ten percent work outside their homes. Eighteen percent held jobs before they were married but became housewives immediately thereafter. Most of the women moved directly from their parents' homes (where they helped their mothers with the younger children and the housework) to their own homes. Sixty-one percent reported having their marriage arranged for them by their parents.

The women's descriptions of their husbands' jobs match closely the occupations reported by the men in the survey. Seventy percent of the husbands work as skilled or unskilled laborers. (Eighty percent of the men who were in the labor force said that they had worked as skilled or unskilled laborers.) Forty percent were unable to say where their husbands were employed or by whom; and 25 percent did not know how much money their husbands earned. Those who did, reported their husbands as earning somewhat less than the men themselves had reported in their interview.

The differences shown in Table 5.4 could easily be attributed to ignorance on the part of the wives. But it is probably more reasonable to assume that wives whose husbands are in the lower portion of the income continuum are less likely to know how much money their husbands earn; and therefore if the husbands' responses could have been solicited directly the differences might have been lessened.

Thirty-three percent of the women said that their family received financial help on a regular basis. The major source of help was their own grown children, not the government.

Table 5.4. *Husbands' monthly earnings reported by wives and husbands*

Monthly earnings	Fathers' responses about income (%)	Mothers' responses about husbands' incomes[a] (%)
Less than 500 I.L. per month	25	40
Between 500 and 700 I.L. per month	32	28
Between 700 and 1000 I.L. per month	42	32

[a]The 25 percent who said they did not know how much money their husbands earned are not included in these percentages.

All except 4 percent speak Arabic exclusively at home. On other occasions, such as when they are shopping, 66 percent use Hebrew and a few speak French. None reported speaking English.

Only 30 percent of the women read a newspaper regularly; that probably includes the entire group who are literate enough to read. All of them listen to the radio for several hours a day to programs in Arabic. One-third do not watch televion regularly because they do not own their own sets. Like the men, those who watch prefer programs in Arabic exclusively.

Eighty-eight percent of the women vote in the national elections. Like the men, the proportion of women in the survey who report that they vote matches the national figures for the Arab community in Israel. Thirty-seven percent refused to reveal the party of their choice. Among those willing to tell us for which party they voted, the Labor Alignment received 82 percent of their votes.

In general, the Arab mothers were approving and uncritical of parent-child relations and of child rearing in their own community and in the larger Jewish society. As the percentages in Table 5.5 demonstrate, the style of dress, and the relations between the sexes (for example, that boys and girls attend the same school in most Jewish Israeli communities), are behaviors about which more women expressed their disapproval than about any of the other topics.

Their judgments about adult behavior in the Jewish Israeli sector, as shown in Table 5.6, are also generally approving; however, 40 percent of them were critical of the relations between the sexes because they perceive women behaving in a way that they regard as loose and immoral.

Like the men, the women are not joiners of organizations. Only 18 percent belong to any type of formal group; and almost always the group is religious in its purpose. Like the ultra-Orthodox Jewish women, the Arab mothers are likely to have four or five young children at home to look after, plus the responsibility of doing all of the housework. Such a schedule is not conducive to volunteer work.

The Arab women are not unaware of the fact that their life is difficult and that there are other women who have an easier time. This perception comes through most clearly when they are asked about what aspects of their life they would live in the same manner and what aspects they would live differently. Only 25 percent opted to live their life essentially as they had. The other 75 percent mentioned specific areas

Table 5.5. *Arab mothers' opinions about behaviors and beliefs in their own community versus the larger society (percentages)*

	Within own community	The rest of society
How parents rear their children		
Approve	94	78
Disapprove	4	20
No opinion	2	2
Education children receive		
Approve	96	96
Disapprove	2	2
No opinion	2	2
Style of dress		
Approve	80	55
Disapprove	20	43
No opinion	—	2
Relations between the sexes		
Approve	71	53
Disapprove	27	45
No opinion	2	2
Ritual and religious observances		
Approve	91	88
Disapprove	9	10
No opinion	—	2

in which they would like to make important changes. All of them would like to have more comfort and more ease. With more money, they believe they could have had a better life. Thirty-three percent said that they would have had fewer children; and 25 percent wanted ''better'' husbands. By that they mean they want husbands who would treat them with more dignity, who would help them more with the children, and who would provide them with more money for themselves and for making their homes more comfortable.

In sum, we have seen that the Arab parents, the mothers as much as the fathers, are aware of their economically depressed situation and of the improvement that more money and more education and better

Table 5.6. *Arab mothers' opinions about behaviors in the larger society (percentages)*

How people spend their time	
Approve	84
Disapprove	14
No opinion	2
Attention given to religious observances	
Approve	69
Disapprove (too little emphasis)	20
No opinion	1
Relations between the sexes	
Approve	59
Disapprove (too loose, women are too free, immoral)	24
Disapprove (not traditional)	16
No opinion	1

jobs could make toward giving them a better life. Unlike the men, the women expressed criticism of their spouses for some of their hardships. Both thought that having smaller families would give each member more comfort and improve their standard of living.

The sons

All of the sons were born in Israel and have lived all of their lives in a Jewish state, surrounded by unfriendly, independent Arab nations. Practically all of the sons are living in the same neighborhood in which they were born.

Forty-eight percent of the boys were attending school at the time of the survey. Most of them are in their eleventh or twelfth years of school. Sixty-seven percent attend Arab schools; the others attend state vocational training schools that have both Arab and Jewish students. The latter said that they expected to remain in school until they have completed their specific course or program of study. Two-thirds of those in the Arab schools said that they plan to go on to the university and study law or medicine. The fact that these respondents are still in school past the compulsory tenth grade and that they are in schools in which they can prepare for the college entrance examinations makes these responses more than mere fantasies. Law and medicine are popular professions among Israeli Arabs, and both types of schools may be entered upon graduation from secondary school. They are also areas of work in which security clearance is not a major stumbling block.

The highest grade completed among those no longer in school was the twelfth. Most had stopped at the end of the eighth year. Over 90 percent are employed as laborers (skilled and unskilled) by private businesses. Their average earning is 400 I.L. per month. Only 10 percent earn over 500 I.L.

Practically all (93 percent) of the sons speak exclusively Arabic at home. But at school or at work, 47 percent use Hebrew exclusively, 23 percent use both Hebrew and Arabic, and 30 percent use only Arabic. On other occasions 37 percent use English in talking with tourists or on various business ventures.

Forty-six percent read a newspaper regularly; and they read the Hebrew press. Practically all of them listen to many different types of programs on the radio, both in Arabic and Hebrew. Seventy-five percent have television sets at home; and they watch only programs in Arabic that originate within Israel and/or come from Jordan, Syria, and Egypt.

All except 4 percent said that they vote or plan to vote in the national elections; but about half refused to indicate for which party. Among those who were willing to name the party they prefer, about 90 percent said that they plan to or usually vote for the Labor Alignment. Ten percent named Rakah as the party of their choice. Unwillingness to reveal the party for which they have voted, or are likely to vote, leads to the speculation that these respondents are supporters of Rakah. As the percentages in Table 3.4 indicate, it is the party that receives a large proportion of the urban Arab vote. Among the boys, it appears that as many as 50 percent might be supporters of Rakah.

Only 4 percent said that they expected to serve in the army. An additional 8 percent do not expect to serve but believe that the Israeli government should make it more attractive for Arabs to serve, thereby providing Arab youth with an opportunity to show their loyalty to Israel. For example, Arabs might be trained for noncombat types of activities. The other 88 percent said that they would not serve even if conditions were more attractive because they do not want to have to fight other Arabs or help in any way an army that was fighting the armies of Arab nations.

The boys' accounts of how they are most likely to spend their time when they are not in school or at work are much like the responses that American or European boys might give. At least two-thirds of them said they spend their time with friends, talking, wandering around the city, and playing ball. The others said they read or spend time with their families.

The extent to which the Arab and Jewish communities are segregated socially, even in those cities in which members of both communities live adjacent to each other, is shown dramatically by the boys' responses to the items that asked them to describe their three closest friends. Only 9 percent said that any of their three closest friends is Jewish. This is true even among those boys who were still in schools in which they might have Jewish classmates. The boys' choice of friends was dictated primarily by ethnicity and school. For example, about 40 percent reported close friends who live in the same city whom they knew from or in school but who do not live in the same neighborhood. The boys who are no longer at school have to arrange to meet them; they are not simply "around" or on the street.

Only 5 percent of the boys were engaged to be married at the time of the survey. Half of the others said they do not plan to marry until they are at least twenty-five years old. When they are ready to marry, 85 percent expect that they alone will decide who their bride will be. They expect their parents' involvement to be minimal. They also expect to set up their own households, not necessarily in the same neighborhood as their parents, but most likely in the same city.

The boys showed little reluctance or embarrassment at discussing the number of children they wanted or expected to father. Only 2 percent, for example, refused to answer the question. Only 1 percent said they would like to have as many children as their wife could bear, and another 1 percent said they did not want any children. The modal response was four children, then three, then two. Only 2 percent wanted one child, and 9 percent wanted more than four. The distribution of responses as to the number of children they would "like to have" was almost identical to the distribution of answers given concerning what they thought "they would have." In both distributions, the modal number and the average number is smaller than the number their parents have.

Fifty-nine percent said that they had no preferences concerning the ratio of boys to girls; but 36 percent wanted more boys than girls, and

5 percent wanted only sons. Their response on the matter of preference for boys over girls reflects the traditions of their parents and their culture more than their response about the number of children they want.

Unlike their fathers, the sons plan to involve themselves in the affairs of the community. Eighty percent said that they expect to be active in organizations that work with young people in sports and in education when they are adults.

The maxim "like father like son" does not appear to be applicable to the urban Arab community. When the boys were asked at the end of the interview whether they approve of their fathers' way of life, whether they plan to follow in their fathers' footsteps, or whether they have a different type of life in mind for themselves, 76 percent were critical and disapproving of their fathers' ways. The targets of their criticism were (and they are given in the order in which the largest proportion of respondents mentioned them): My father had more children than he could provide for; he does not try hard enough to earn a better living for his family; he did not prepare his children for modern living; and he should be more active in community and civic affairs. The sons appear more interested in the affairs and activities of the larger society. They are also more ambitious than their fathers. At the same time, they are committed to maintaining a separate and visible Arab identity as witness their reactions to the prospect of serving in the Israeli army and, according to our guess, the political party that many of them support.

The daughters

Like the sons, the daughters are native-born Israelis. Eighty-six percent have lived in the same neighborhood since birth, and all but 2 percent have lived in their present neighborhood for at least ten years. They range in age from sixteen to twenty-one, the modal age being twenty.

Thirty-seven percent of the girls were attending school at the time of the survey. All except 15 percent of the others were working outside their homes. The jobs they hold involve more skill and have more prestige than those reported by the boys. The girls are either teachers or are employed as clerks or salespersons or are engaged in a skilled craft. Most of them report that the decision to take a job was their own, but that their parents did not object to their doing so. The salaries they receive, however, are lower than those reported by the boys. The mode is 300 I.L. per month, and only 2 percent earn more than 500 I.L. per month.

Among the girls who are still attending school, 25 percent have not completed the compulsory tenth grade; 55 percent are in their eleventh and twelfth years of school; and 20 percent have completed high school and are attending a two-year teachers' seminary. Two-thirds of those who are no longer in school had completed at least the twelfth grade, and a few had gone on to a teachers' seminary. The others had dropped out earlier. The reasons most often given by the girls for no longer being in school were that they had finished their course of study or that they were needed at home for financial reasons. More than half of the girls said that they would like to go back to school and enroll eventually in a college or university; but they are not clear about what their major area of study would be. The daughters seem to have higher educational and occupational aspirations than the sons in a culture in which women have traditionally played a subservient role.

Like the boys, most of the girls speak only Arabic in their homes. But also like the boys, all of them are comfortable in at least one other language: Hebrew and/or English for two-thirds, and French for the other third. Ten percent claim that they use Hebrew in speaking with their friends, which suggests that 10 percent have Jewish friends. Indeed, when the girls were asked directly about their friends, only about 10 percent said that one of their three closest friends was not an Arab. Most of their friends had been or are classmates.

The girls are more avid consumers of the mass media than are the boys. Three-quarters read a newspaper regularly; two-thirds read the Arabic press, and one-third the Hebrew press. All but 4 percent listen to the radio, and most of them listen to all types of programs, for many hours in the day. Two-thirds have a television set at home on which they watch only programs in Arabic.

Ninety-eight percent of the girls vote or expect to vote in the national elections, but 52 percent refused to say which party they support. Among those who indicated their preference, four out of five said the Labor Alignment; the others named Rakah.

Twelve percent of the girls were engaged at the time of the survey. Half of them said that their parents had selected their prospective husbands for them. Among those who were not engaged, three-quarters expected to make the choice on their own; and the others expected that their parents and/or some relatives would initiate the arrangements but would leave them a veto option. Most of them expected to be married by the time they were twenty-three; the modal age was twenty-one.

The girls showed no embarrassment or resistance when answering the questions concerning the number of children they wanted and thought they would have. The distribution of their responses shows that 84 percent do not want more than four children; and 55 percent want three or fewer. These numbers, if realized, would represent a sharp drop in the Israeli Arab birth rate. Only 4 percent said that they would have as many as they could or as many as their husbands wanted. Equally interesting, because it is nontraditional, is the fact that two-thirds said that they would like the same number of boys as girls. There was only 6 percent preference for boys over girls.

Unlike the sons, who were critical of their fathers, the daughters were more loath to express disapproval or criticism of their mothers' way of life when asked to do so directly. For example, when they were asked to indicate which aspects of their mothers' lives they approved and would like to emulate, 60 percent said they were wholly approving and would not criticize any aspect of their mothers' way of living. The 40 percent who were willing to express criticism disapproved most of all of the number of children their mothers had and, second, of their mothers' lack of education, and narrowness of interests.

These responses, plus the ones made about selecting their husbands, the number of children they expect to have, and their educational and occupational aspirations, suggest that significant social changes may be occurring in the life style and social roles of the young Arab women. Further discussion of the meaning of these changes may be found in Chapters 7 and 9.

6. Sex role characteristics in the ultra–Orthodox family

These next two chapters pick up where Chapters 4 and 5 have left off. They describe the families in each of the two communities by focusing on the similarities and differences in attitudes, beliefs, and behaviors that are a function of sex roles within both the parents' and the children's generations. This chapter describes the ultra-Orthodox community; Chapter 7 describes the urban Arab community.

We expected that the women in Mea Shearim, both the mothers and the daughters, would be more open to change and less critical of the larger society than the fathers and sons because it is the women who are obliged to have more contact with the larger society in their day-to-day lives and because the ultra-Orthodox community makes fewer provisions for insulating them from the larger culture. These characteristics were true of women in the shtetls in Eastern Europe, and we anticipated that they would generalize to this community.

The schools that the women attend, for example, do not remain in session all day, and in the evening as well. Nor are the women expected to attend school for as many years as the men. The decision not to serve in the army is not as critical for the women as it is for the men; and, therefore, it is not as likely to result in the development of strongly negative beliefs about the larger culture and the importance of separating themselves from it. The men also are more likely to see themselves as having greater responsibility for the continuity of the ultra-Orthodox community and therefore are stricter about preventing contamination of their bodies as well as their minds and souls by contact with the larger society.

Mothers' and fathers' roles

About 60 percent of the parents were born in Israel. Those who were not came from Eastern Europe. There is no difference between the mothers and the fathers concerning the period in which they migrated to Israel. More of the fathers than the mothers have lived in the same neighborhood either from birth, or for more than twenty-five years. This difference reflects the process whereby the bride is more likely to move into the neighborhood of her husband's family, so that the husband can continue to study at the same yeshiva that he has been with before marriage with as little disruption of his daily routine as possible. The fathers tend to be somewhat older than the mothers; 38 percent of the fathers are over fifty compared with 26 percent of the mothers.

The most dramatic difference between the mothers and fathers is in the amount of education each received. The percentages are presented in Table 6.1. Seventy-four percent of the mothers received less than an eighth-grade education, whereas 45 percent of the fathers attended school for more than sixteen years (probably for all of their lives from the time they were three years old).

There is no overlap in the occupations of the men and women, since 93 percent of the women are housewives. Forty-four percent of the men hold jobs that are connected with religious education or adminis-tration, and 45 percent of the women describe their husband's jobs as being of the same type. About the same proportion, 54 percent of the women and 55 percent of the men, refused to say how much they (or their spouse) earned. Among those who did indicate an amount, there was little difference in the distributions; 55 percent of the men and 65 percent of the women said between 500 and 1,000 I.L. per month. We

Table 6.1. *Mothers' and fathers' years of schooling (percentages)*

	Number of years of schooling				
	None	Up to 8 years[a]	9–12 years	13–16 years[b]	More than 16 years
Mothers	4	70	16	8	2
Fathers	2	10	15	28	45

[a]Eight percent of the mothers and 4 percent of the fathers in this category said that they attended a "nonreligious" school.

[b]Half of the mothers in this category attended nonreligious schools.

reported in Chapter 4 that the average salary for the urban Israeli family that has at least six children is 947 I.L.

Sixty-six percent of both the men and the women said that they received no financial help on a regular basis from any source; and 18 percent of the fathers and 10 percent of the mothers did not answer the question. Given the incomes reported and the size of the families, plus the existence of a large number of organizations whose main job it is to help families in which the fathers and/or sons are devoting themselves to the study of Torah, the large proportion who deny receiving any financial help is doubtful. Most of those who did acknowledge that they receive help said that their help came from the yeshivas or from other religious organizations. The government, friends, and relatives, were mentioned by 33 percent of the fathers and 25 percent of the mothers.

The language usage patterns of the men and women are quite different. For example, 80 percent of the men compared with 36 percent of the women, reported that they speak only Yiddish at home. Most of the women claimed they use several languages in their homes: Hebrew, Yiddish, Hungarian, Polish and so on. Only 3 percent of the men, compared with 16 percent of the women, reported speaking any other European language. When the location shifted from the home to the street, we found that the men spoke Hebrew more often than the women, but that the women were more likely to use Hungarian, Russian, Polish, and other Eastern European languages.

One explanation for the difference in the patterns of language usage is that among those respondents who were born in the shtetls of Eastern and Central Europe, the women, both in the schools they attended and in their day-to-day activities, were more likely to be exposed to the larger culture, where the language was Polish, Russian, or Hungarian, but not Yiddish; the men on the other hand spent most of their time in the yeshivas, where the language was Yiddish.

Even in Israel there are more effective mechanisms for insulating the men than the women. When their sons are three years old, the parents are likely to send them to talmud torahs, where the language of instruction is Yiddish. A boy is likely to remain in Yiddish-speaking schools until he is married or indeed all of his life. The hours he sits in school per day may extend until five or six in the evening or, for the older boys, until ten or eleven at night. The ultra-Orthodox girls are not expected to begin school as early as the boys, nor are they expected to remain in school for as many hours per day, nor to study for as many years. When they are not in school, they are expected to help manage the affairs of the family. These affairs cannot help but involve them in excursions into the larger society, where Hebrew is the spoken language.

The difference between the men's and women's language usage is comparable to their differential exposure to the mass media. Just as the women are more likely to use the language of the larger culture than are the men, so are they also more likely to read newspapers, and to read those papers that reflect a more secular perspective. They are also more likely to listen to the radio. Forty-six percent of the women, compared with 19 percent of the men, read a Hebrew secular paper and at least one newspaper that is printed in a European language. Compared with 39 percent of the women, 70 percent of the men who read a newspaper regularly read only *Hamodia* (the organ of the Agudat Party) or *Shearim* (the organ of the Poale Agudat, i.e., Orthodox workers' party).

Fifty-five percent of the men, compared with 36 percent of the women, do not listen to the radio. The women, of course, are likely to be at home all day and therefore if a radio is permitted in the house, they would have more time to listen. It is interesting that although 36 percent of the women do not listen, less than half of them gave as their reason for not doing so that it was "forbidden." Among the men, all of the 53 percent save one said that they did not listen to the radio because it is forbidden according to their beliefs. Most of the women who listen to the radio listen to all types of programs: stories, music, news, and so on.

Although practically none of the men or women watch television (2 and 10 percent, respectively), only 22 percent of the women, compared with 44 percent of the men, gave as their reason that "it was forbidden by religious law."

On the matter of whether they vote, 32 percent of the women and 38 percent of the men said that they do not; but over 80 percent of the men, compared with 33 percent of the women, gave as their reason for not doing so that they are opposed to and do not recognize the legitimacy of the state. Among the men and women who do vote, there was no difference in their party preferences. Practically all of them said that they vote for the Agudat Party. As the voting statistics described in Chapter 3 indicate, over 80 percent of the Israeli public vote in the national elections. The Agudat Party has consistently been represented in the Knesset by four members, which indicates that the party receives about 3 percent of the national vote. Most of it comes from Jerusalem.

The men's and women's responses to the questions about language usage, mass media exposure, and voting behavior confirm our belief that the women in Mea Shearim are both more influenced by and more exposed to "outside" influences. They are less "pure types" than are the men of their generation.

By and large, neither the mothers nor the fathers belong to formal groups or organizations. Among the one-third of the fathers who claimed membership in a formal association, religious and philanthropic groups and political organizations are the two types preferred.

The fathers and mothers are in general agreement about how children in Mea Shearim are being and should be reared and their subsequent behavior. Over 80 percent approve of the education their children receive, their style of dress, their relations between the sexes, and their religious observances. The one area in which there is disagreement between the mothers and fathers and in which 61 percent of the fathers disapprove, compared with 10 percent of the mothers, concerns the manner in which children relate to their parents. The fathers believe that the children do not show enough respect for their parents and that the parents do not exercise enough authority over their children. On the other hand, both the mothers and fathers were almost unanimous in their disapproval of the practices of the larger society vis-à-vis children.

Reactions to adult behavior in the larger society also reflected near-consensus of opinion between the mothers and the fathers. They agreed that the life style of most Israelis is decadent and immoral. Whenever there was any disagreement between the mothers and the fathers — whether it was in regard to the children or the adults — it was always the women who were less negative than the men. For example, 16 percent of the women, compared with 3 percent of the men, said they approved of the extent of the religious and ritual observances among "other Israelis," and 12 percent of the women, compared with 2 percent of the men, approved of the education that children in the larger society receive.

In the portion of the interview that focused on their adolescent children, 92 percent of the fathers and 66 percent of the mothers were talking about a child who was still in school. The sons tended to be further along than the daughters: Eighty-five percent of the boys, compared with 28 percent of the girls, had completed at least twelve years of school. Sixteen percent of the daughters and 25 percent of the sons were engaged to be married at the time of the survey. When the mothers and fathers of those not engaged were asked about how their sons' or daughters' spouses will be selected, 20 percent of the mothers, compared with 7 percent of the fathers, said that their child would choose his or her own mate.

In general, neither the mothers nor the fathers reported disagreements nor anticipated that disagreements would occur in the future between themselves and their children on issues such as how the children spend their time when they are not at school, their choice of friends, their style of dress, and the extent of their religious observances.

When the parents were asked to think ahead a few years and indicate whether they expected their married sons' or daughters' lives to be similar or different from their own, most of them indicated that they expected that their children would follow their life style and emulate their values. When there was a difference, however, it was the mothers rather than the fathers who were more likely to anticipate it. For example, 60 percent of the mothers, compared with 86 percent of the fathers, expected their daughters to rear their children as they had been reared.

Finally, and in sum, in Table 6.2 we compare the mothers' and

Table 6.2. *Ultra-Orthodox mothers' and fathers' responses to: If you had a chance to live your life over again?*

Responses	Mother (%)	Father (%)
Everything is predetermined; therefore cannot or will not answer.	10	8
Essentially the same.	58	32
Mostly the same; but would like more time for Torah study and prayer.	—	45
Mostly the same; but would like more ease and comfort in my life.	30	—
Mostly the same; but would like fewer children.	2	—
Mostly the same; but would like a chance to learn a trade and better financial circumstances.	—	15

fathers' responses to the question with which we concluded each of the interviews: "If you had a chance to live your life over again, what aspects of it would you live the same and what aspects would you live differently?" Fifty-eight percent of the women, compared with 32 percent of the men, said that they would not change any aspect of their lives. But, when the responses of those who would make some changes are compared, 75 percent of the men wish their lives to be devoted still more to prayer and religious studies and to be isolated to a greater degree from the concerns of day-to-day activities. Among the women who opted for changes, all of them wanted an easier, more comfortable life.

In sum, then, there is in the mothers' responses, as opposed to the fathers', a persistent although not strong theme that suggests more willingness to change, a greater exposure to and a greater receptiveness of some aspects of the larger culture, and a less doctrinaire approach to their own lives and those of their daughters.

Sons and daughters

The preceding discussion has shown that the ultra-Orthodox mothers are somewhat less committed to the past and to a strictly orthodox interpretation of traditions than the fathers. In this section the attitudes, perceptions, and behaviors of the sons and daughters who have not yet established families of their own are compared for the purpose of answering the following questions: Does the somewhat greater flexibility and openness that was observed on the part of the older women extend into the next generation? Do the daughters have more contact with the larger society? Are they less hostile and rejecting of the dominant culture? And are they more likely than the sons to interact with the larger society as they become more independent of their parents?

In contrast to the mothers and fathers, about 40 percent of whom were born in the ghettos and shtetls of Eastern Europe, all of the daughters and sons were born in Israel since its establishment as an independent Jewish state. They were also all born in Jerusalem; and almost all of them have lived in Mea Shearim for at least the past ten years of their lives.

Ninety-two percent of the sons were still attending yeshivas, and 66 percent of the girls were still in school at the time of the survey. Of the girls who are no longer in school, 45 percent had attended until tenth grade or less. The others had attended a teachers' seminary for two years following their graduation from secondary school.

In their use of language, the sons follow their fathers, and the daughters their mothers. For example, 45 percent of the girls, compared with 6 percent of the boys, said they speak Hebrew exclusively at home; and 80 percent of the boys, compared with 2 percent of the girls, said they speak Yiddish exclusively. If one was to guess what the common language is when sons and mothers talk to each other and when daughters and fathers speak to each other, Yiddish would be the likely choice, since the males are the dominant participants, even when they are much younger than the females. The fact that the daughters said that they speak Hebrew exclusively at home probably indicates that there are relatively few cross-sex conversations, especially between fathers and daughters. Over 80 percent of the sons and daughters use other languages, mostly Hebrew, Polish, and Hungarian when the occasion demands, such as at government agencies.

The boys' as well as the girls' closest friends are adolescents whom they met at school and who come from the same type of families that they do. Many more of the boys than the girls said that their best friends live in the same neighborhood. But that is probably a function of the fact that there are more yeshivas located in other parts of Jerusalem and families living outside of Mea Shearim do not have to send their sons to a yeshiva in Mea Shearim. Ultra-Orthodox families have fewer choices where their daughters are concerned. They must send them to schools in Mea Shearim if they want them to receive an ultra-Orthodox education in a private, non-Agudat school. About 10 percent of the girls in contrast to 1 or 2 percent of the boys described friends who came from families that are not as religious as the respondent.

One of the big differences between the sons and daughters was revealed in their comments about their exposure to the mass media and their expectations about voting. Like their mothers, the daughters are much more likely to read a newspaper regularly; 71 percent of the girls, compared with 26 percent of the boys, said that they did. Among them, a higher proportion of the girls read a Hebrew-language secular paper than do the boys. They are also much more likely to listen to the radio — 33 percent versus 74 percent. Those who do not listen are less likely to give as their reasons that their religious beliefs forbid it — 6 percent versus 53 percent. The same pattern is repeated for television watching, save that practically no one watches TV. But 50 percent of the boys, compared with 6 percent of the girls, gave as their reason for not watching TV that it is forbidden by the laws of their religion.

Forty-four percent of the boys, compared with 75 percent of the girls, vote or plan to vote in the national elections. Among those who do not vote, 50 percent of the girls, compared with 80 percent of the boys, said they do not vote because they do not recognize the legitimacy of the state.

Less than 25 percent of the adolescents were engaged to be married at the time of the survey. In almost all instances among those who are engaged, a professional matchmaker and their parents were involved in the selection of the future spouse and in the subsequent arrangements. Those who are not engaged anticipated that the selection and all of the subsequent arrangements would be made in the same manner.

As we saw earlier, the topic that aroused the most resistance and caused the greatest embarrassment among the boys concerned the number of children they would like to have and the number they thought they would have. The boys were more resistant than the girls to any discussion of this topic. Fifty percent of the boys, compared with 15 percent of the girls, refused to answer any of the questions on this topic; but almost all of the boys as well as girls refused to state a number. In place of a number their answers were "as many as I can," "as many as my husband wants," "as many as God will give me." Only 20 percent of the boys and 10 percent of the girls specified a number on the "would have" question, and 29 percent of the girls and 26 percent of the boys specified a number on the "like to have" version. Their responses to the item that asked about the ratio of boys to girls or vice versa evoked the same level of response; 66 percent of the girls and 72 percent of the boys refused to say what ratio of boys to girls they would like to have. Among the few who did answer, two-thirds of the girls said they would like to have the same number of boys as girls. All but two of the boys said they would prefer more sons than daughters.

No significant differences were found in the proportions of boys or girls who said they had disagreements with their fathers or mothers on issues such as how they spend their time, their choice of friends, and their style of dress. On each issue fewer than 15 percent mentioned having any disagreements. The same pattern prevailed in the similarity of the sons' and daughters' responses to questions that asked them to compare their lives after they were married with those of their mothers or fathers. Almost all of them anticipated that they would act and live as their parents do.

The question that evoked more surprise than any of the others (and some resentment) was the last one: "Do you approve or disapprove of your father's (mother's) way of life?" About 80 percent of the daughters and 90 percent of the sons said they approved fully of their parents' way of life and wanted to follow it without making any alterations, improvements, or variations on it. Among the few who disapproved, all of the daughters were critical of their mothers for not having enough outside interests, for not having enough education, and for being too subservient to their husbands. Among the even smaller group of sons who disapproved, as many were critical of their fathers for not being "observant enough" as thought he was too removed from the "modern, real world."

In sum, many of the differences between the sons and daughters that may be attributed to their sex roles were smaller than were those observed between the fathers and the mothers. But the direction of the differences appears to be the same. The daughters show some of the same signs as their mothers, that they are more open to change and to influence from the larger culture than are their brothers. But because they are younger, and because they live under their parents' roof and control, the girls seem more passive and more traditional than their mothers. Of course not until they marry and establish their own households will they be in a position to have more extensive contacts with the larger society through shopping, medical care for their children, social welfare services for those willing to accept them, and the responsibility for acting as a representative of their family. Marriage brings about greater changes in the role and status of girls than it does for boys. In many instances, the boy will continue to function in his dominant role, that of a yeshiva student for most of his adult life.

In that stage of their lives in which we observed them, the young girls do not appear significantly different from their brothers of the same generation. Their greater exposure to the mass media, their more extensive use of Hebrew, and their plans to vote in the national elections are the exceptions.

7. Sex role characteristics in the urban Arab family

This chapter parallels the previous one in that it describes attitudes, perceptions, and behavior as functions of the respondent's sex role within each of the generations among members of the Israeli urban Arab community.

Our expectations for this community were that the sons would be more critical of their fathers than the daughters would be of their mothers, and that the sons would be more anxious to discard some of the traditional aspects of Arab culture such as time spent in the coffee-houses, and style of dress. The sons, we expected, would also be more desirous of achieving the symbols of success that are sought by Jewish Israelis, namely, higher education and occupational prestige. Unlike the ultra-Orthodox community, among the Arabs it is the men who have the more extensive contacts with the larger society in their jobs, at school, and in their dealings with the governmental bureaucracy. The women are expected to remain at home looking after their children, their husbands, and the upkeep of their homes.

We thought that the differences between the mothers and daughters would not be as great, although we anticipated changes of the same type as those that we expected to see between the sons and the fathers. Thus we anticipated greater convergence between the adolescent respondents than between the mothers and the fathers in matters of tastes, interests, and aspirations. The daughters' educational and occupational plans, for example, would be closer to those of their brothers than to those of their mothers; and the difference between the mothers' and the fathers' roles would be greater than the differences between the sons' and the daughters'.

Mothers and fathers

More than 90 percent of both the mothers and the fathers were born in that portion of Palestine that became Israel in 1948. The only difference in the origins of the two samples is that more of the men were born in

121

Jaffa than in Haifa; and for the women it was the other way around. There was no greater likelihood, however, that one group or the other was born in a village and migrated to the city as children or adults. Practically all of the men and the women have lived in the same neighborhood for at least the last fifteen years; about half of them have lived there from birth. The male respondents tended to be somewhat older than the females, as the distribution in Table 7.1 indicates.

Twice as many mothers as fathers never attended school — 29 percent versus 15 percent. Among the others, 59 percent of the mothers attended school for eight years or less, and 12 percent for more than eight years; 60 percent of the fathers attended for eight years or less, and 25 percent attended for several years longer.

There was no overlapping in the mothers' and fathers' occupations: all but two of the mothers are housewives. The jobs that the women reported their husbands held matched closely the jobs reported by the male respondents, as shown in Table 7.2.

Table 7.1. *Age distribution of Arab mothers and fathers*

Age	Men (%)	Women (%)
Over 70	5	—
50–69	36	27
45–49	26	18
40–44	23	29
Less than 40	7	26

Table 7.2. *Fathers' and husbands' occupations*

Occupational categories	Fathers' response (%)	Mothers' responses (about husbands) (%)
Professional	5.6	3.6
Merchant/businessman	2.4	2.0
Sales/white collar	7.6	9.8
Skilled	32.3	27.5
Unskilled	33.1	27.5
Other, retired, unemployed	18.6	10.0
Don't know/no answer	—	19.3
Total	99.6	100.0

The womens' estimates of how much money their husbands were paid were lower than the average wages reported by the male respondents about themselves. For example 75 percent of the men who answered the income question (18 percent did not answer) said they earned between 500 and 1000 I.L. per month; in contrast to 52 percent of the women who claimed that their husbands' monthly wages were between 500 and 1000 I.L. Twenty-three percent said that they earned less than 500 I.L. per month. Twenty-five percent of the women said they did not know what their husbands' earnings were; none refused to answer and none indicated that they felt the question was too delicate.

Since 19 percent of the women could not describe what kind of work their husbands did for a living and 39 percent said they did not know where their husbands worked, we think their responses to the income question should be taken as indicative of the state of their information. The wife's ignorance of the family's financial status may be illustrative of a strict separation of sex role responsibilities within these families that may not carry over into the next generation.

Along these same lines, 63 percent of the women, compared with 40 percent of the men, said that their families did not receive any financial assistance on a regular basis. The government was the chief source of assistance for those families who said they were receiving some type of regular financial help. Again, it is reasonable to assume that many of the women are not aware of the various sources and amounts of money that are available to the family; especially if the funds come in the form of union welfare benefits, their husbands would be even more likely to be the recipients and managers of those funds.

Ninety-six percent of the men and women speak only Arabic at home; outside their homes about 17 percent of the men and women use Hebrew for business, shopping, and contacts with the government. Fourteen percent of the women reported that they speak Hebrew with their "friends" (suggesting thereby that they have Jewish friends), but none of the men said that they used Hebrew in conversations with friends. Thirty percent of the men, and none of the women, reported using English for business or other purposes.

Belonging to clubs or organizations is not common among either the men or the women as represented by the responses of 78 percent of the women and 61 percent of the men who said that they do not belong to any formal groups. Among the men who do belong, membership is most likely to be in a labor union.

The mothers and fathers do not differ in any significant manner in their exposure to the mass media. Between 65 and 70 percent of both the men and women said they do not read a newspaper regularly. Among the minority who do, the women read an Arabic-language paper almost exclusively, but the men are divided about evenly between those who exclusively read newspapers in Arabic and those who read a Hebrew paper as well. Listening to the radio is equally popular with the men and women, save that the women listen for more hours per day, which is probably a function of their being at home all day. Twenty-five percent of the men listen to the news and other programs in Hebrew as well as Arabic, compared with 8 percent of the women. The others listen only to programs in Arabic. Two-thirds of the women and three-fourths of the men report owning television sets. About half of them owned sets before television was introduced in Israel. Twenty-one percent of the fathers, compared with 4 percent of the mothers, watch Hebrew as well as Arabic-language programs, whereas the others watch only programs in Arabic.

Their voting patterns are also similar in that almost all of them (except 10 percent of the women and 3 percent of the men) reported that they vote in the national elections. Among those who would tell us for which party they voted (63 percent of the women and 78 percent of the men), the Labor Party was the choice of 90 percent of the fathers and 84 percent of the mothers. About 10 percent said they voted for Rakah candidates. Assuming that most of the respondents who refused to indicate the party they supported voted for Rakah, we find that the Labor Alignment would still receive a majority of the votes among both the mothers and the fathers.

The responses of the mothers and fathers to child-rearing practices and to relations between parents and children within their own community revealed a consistent pattern: The men are less approving than the women, although both groups registered higher percentages of approval than disapproval. The distributions are shown in Table 7.3.

The fathers who disapproved said in essence that the children are not respectful enough of their parents, that they dress in an immoral and indecent manner, that the boys and girls spend too much time together, and that the education they receive does not adequately prepare them for adult life in Israeli society. Interestingly, however, when the fathers were asked whether they approved of these qualities and characteristics in Jewish children, fewer of them registered disapproval; and the differ-

Table 7.3. *Arab fathers' and mothers' opinions about behaviors and beliefs in their own community*

	Approval of own community (%)	
Categories	Men	Women
Parent-children relationship	66	94
Education children receive	62	96
Style of dress	58	80
Relations between the sexes	62	71
Religious observances	76	91

Table 7.4. *Arab fathers' and mothers' opinions about behaviors and beliefs in the larger society*

	Approval of the larger society (%)	
Categories	Men	Women
Parent-children relationship	81	78
Education children receive	94	96
Style of dress	53	55
Relations between the sexes	70	53
Religious observances	75	88

ence between the mothers and fathers did not follow any consistent pattern.

A comparison of the responses about their own community and about the larger society (see Table 7.4) indicates that the fathers are more critical of relations between parents and children, of the education Arab children receive, and to a lesser extent of religious observances and of the relations between the sexes in their own community than in the larger, Jewish, society. The mothers are more approving of such behavior in their own community than in the larger society. But more of the mothers are critical of the style in which most Jewish Israelis dress and of the relations between boys and girls (dimensions that may be readily observed in public) than they are of the other activities.

Concerning adult behavior in the larger society, the highest percentages of disapproval came in response to the question about relations between the sexes. Forty percent of the mothers and the fathers disapproved on grounds that the relations indicate a lack of morality and decency. Fewer fathers than mothers said they approved of the way Jewish Israelis spend their time when they are not working (69 percent vs. 84 percent), but more fathers approved of the degree to which Jewish Israelis observe their religion (85 percent vs. 69 percent). The fathers were critical of the Israelis for being too frivolous, for spending too much time at discotheques and movies; the mothers were disapproving of Israelis for not being more observant of their religion.

In that portion of the interview that focused on the relationship between the parent and the adolescent son or daughter as perceived by the parent, we found that the mothers and fathers offered different explanations for why their son or daughter was no longer in school. (Fifty-two percent of the sons and 63 percent of the daughters were no longer attending school.) Over 70 percent of the mothers said that their daughters had finished their course or had graduated from the school that they had been attending. Over 70 percent of the fathers said of their sons that they were not interested in attending school any longer or that they had to work in order to help the family financially. In fact the girls attended school for more years than the boys. Sixty-five percent of the daughters, compared with 25 percent of the sons, went further than the compulsory ten years and completed secondary school (46 percent) and teachers' seminary (19 percent).

There was little difference as to years in school among those sons and daughters who were still in school. The fact that these are urban Arab families rather than families who live in the villages is crucial. Practically all of the mothers (96 percent) said they approved of their daughters not attending school any longer; but half of the fathers would not answer the question about their sons. Among those who did, over 62 percent said they disapproved of their sons' behavior in not continuing in school.

Hardly any of the adolescents were engaged to be married (12 percent of the daughters and 5 percent of the sons) at the time of the survey. But 78 percent of the mothers said they expected their daughters to be married by the time they were twenty-one. The fathers did not expect their sons to marry until they were at least twenty-five years of age. The pattern whereby the boy is several years older than the girl is traditional among Arab families, in which the future husband is expected to pay the bride's family for allowing him to take her from her family of birth.

Eighty-three percent of the fathers, compared with 43 percent of the mothers, expect that their sons or daughters will decide on their own whom they want to marry and will make the necessary arrangements. Twenty percent of the mothers said they did not know how to answer the question because they could not foresee two or three years into the future on a matter that they knew was undergoing change. If most of the 20 percent who were not able to answer are saying in effect that "it is quite likely that my daughter will make the decision on her own," then there is not much difference between the mothers' and fathers' expectations. Most of them, then, do not expect their son or daughter to follow the traditional procedure.

In response to the questions that asked the fathers and mothers whether they had any disagreements with their sons or daughters about their choice of friends, how they spend their spare time, and so on, we found that only a relatively small proportion of either the mothers or the fathers said that they have had such disagreements. A higher proportion of the fathers said that they have had disagreements with their sons, for example, 30 percent of the fathers, compared with 12 percent of the mothers, on how their sons or daughters spend their spare time. On their choice of friends, 30 percent versus 14 percent said there have been disagreements. On both matters, the fathers who said they have had disagreements with their sons also said that their sons went to the movies, attended discotheques, drank alcoholic beverages, and engaged in other frivolous and immoral activities; and that their sons' friends spent their time in such activities.

When asked to think ahead and indicate whether they expected their sons' or daughters' lives to be similar to or different from their own, 60 percent of both the mothers and the fathers said that they thought their son or daughter would rear his or her children differently and that their children would emphasize different values than they did. Slightly less than half of the mothers and slightly more than half of the fathers expected that their daughters or sons would be as observant as they were about religion. In the mother's case, in most instances that meant that she expected her daughter to be observant. In the father's case, it meant that the son would not be observant. Among those fathers and mothers who anticipated differences between their son's or daughter's practices and their own, the difference was almost always in the direction of the son or daughter being less or not at all observant.

Most of the Arab fathers (85 percent) and mothers (75 percent) said that given the opportunity, they would like to live aspects of their lives differently. The fathers focused on two issues: better economic circumstances, by which they meant a chance to learn a trade, and the choice of having fewer children, for which they could provide better. The women focused on three aspects: an easier life (one with more comforts), a better husband (one who was both more understanding and sympathetic as well as capable of providing a better living for the family), and fewer children. Both the mothers and fathers, in almost the same proportions (one-third of the former and one-fourth of the latter), mentioned smaller families and connected smaller families with improved economic circumstances.

To sum up, we found fewer differences between the roles and attitudes of the Arab mothers and fathers than we had expected; but the differences that we found were in the expected direction. The fathers are more open to and more willing to condone change in their children's lives than are the mothers. The differences between the mothers and fathers stem from the mother's deeper commitment to tradition and Orthodoxy. Since it is the adult males in the Arab community who are likely to establish the tone for the families' observances and life styles, we expect that the Arabs in the cities will move closer to the dominant culture and seek (to the extent that they are welcomed) more extensive contacts with the larger society.

Sons and daughters

We found among the adults that the fathers had greater contacts with the larger society and were more knowledgeable about and accepting of the dominant culture. Between the boys and girls we expected that the differences would be in the same direction but more attenuated. In other words, the sons would be less committed to the traditional culture than the daughters, even though the young Arab women who live in the urban centers, and who have been born since the establishment of the state, may have experienced more rapid changes in their personal lives and in their social environment than have the boys of the same generation. But we believe that these girls still have a longer distance to travel. The changes in the young women's behavior are likely to manifest themselves in areas such as their education, their style of dress, and in the jobs they hold. Given the strong patriarchal quality of Arab society, however, the women are likely to be more insulated and more traditional than the men. Thus when we compared attitudes and behavior within the same generation, we expected to find smaller differences between the sons and daughters than between the mothers and fathers; but those differences that do exist should show that the sons are less insulated and more personally acculturated than the daughters.

All of the sons and daughters were born in Israel, and practically all (over 85 percent) have lived in the same neighborhoods since birth. About the same proportions were no longer in school at the time of the survey (63 percent of the daughters and 54 percent of the sons). When asked why they had stopped going to school, most of the girls said because they had finished their course in contrast to a majority of the boys who said they had stopped attending because they were not interested in school. The mothers and fathers had offered essentially the same explanations. Among those who are employed, the girls work as teachers, clerks, and in handicraft industries. The sons are either skilled or unskilled laborers.

All of the sons and daughters (save seven and two percent) speak exclusively Arabic at home. But on other occasions, Hebrew and/or English is used for business, shopping, and with friends by all of the girls and by 67 percent of the boys. English is used with friends much more than Hebrew, which indicates that their friends are not Jewish.

The close friendships reported by the boys and girls follow a similar pattern. Almost all of them met their friends at school; they come from the same type of families; that is, they are Muslim, and of comparable socioeconomic status. Most of them live in the same city although not in the immediate neighborhood. The latter phenomenon is largely a function of the number and location of schools for Arab children in a given city.

Fifty-four percent of the boys, compared with 25 percent of the girls, do not read a newspaper. Among those who do read a newspaper regularly, 75 percent of the girls read Arabic newspapers and 66 percent of the boys read the Hebrew press. The girls' selection is not a function of language facility. It indicates a real preference. Almost all of them listen to the radio. Most of the boys reported listening for only an hour or so a day, but the girls said they listen for "many" hours. More boys than girls (47 percent vs. 20 percent) said they listen to stories, news, and music in Hebrew as well as Arabic, and more girls prefer Arabic exclusively. At least two-thirds watch television regularly, but again more of the boys (63 percent vs. 42 percent) watch Hebrew-language programs as well as programs in Arabic. More of the girls limit their viewing to programs in Arabic. In sum, in their exposure to the mass media, the boys show more contacts with, and more interest in, the dominant culture than do the girls.

The voting patterns of boys and girls are similar. Fifty-one percent of the boys and 52 percent of the girls claim that they have voted or will vote but refused to indicate for which party. Almost all of the others said that they prefer the labor party, save for 17 percent of the girls and 6 percent of the boys who named Rakah as the party of their choice.

In that portion of the interview that asked about disagreements with parents, over 75 percent of both the boys and girls said that they have had no disagreements on the topics mentioned. But on the matter of whether they expected to rear their children as their parents reared them, and on the strength of their religious commitments, at least half of the sons as well as the daughters anticipated differences in points of view. They claimed that they would emphasize different values and would be more permissive in the rearing of their children. They also expected to be less observant of their religion.

The biggest difference between the sons and daughters occurred in response to the last question asked: Did they approve of their father's or mother's way of life, and did they wish to emulate it? Sixty-one percent of the daughters, compared with 24 percent of the sons, said they approved of their mother's or father's way of life without any qualifications. The daughters who disapproved of their mother's life style or who disapproved of some aspects of it, offered two reasons. They thought that their mothers should have had more outside interests and that they should have had fewer children. For themselves, they plan to have smaller families and they want to be more active in community affairs. The sons disapproved of their father's way of life because he failed to earn the kind of living that could provide adequately for his family, because he had too many children, and because he did not adequately prepare his children for living in the type of society in which they found themselves.

The common denominator in the sons' and daughters' responses is their belief that their parents have had too many children. The sons make a direct connection between family size and lower socioeconomic status. The daughters tend to connect family size and their mother's confinement to the house and lack of interests. Both see the traditional "large family" as an impediment to changes that they wish to bring about in their own lives. The major changes that the sons' responses focus on are those that have value and expression in the dominant culture. They are expressions of a work ethic and an achievement orientation, coupled with smaller families.

In summary, we found that it is the sons who manifest more dramatic signs of change and a greater willingness to accept aspects of the life style and value orientation of the dominant culture. The daughters appear to be moving, albeit more slowly, in the same direction.

8. Sex and generational roles in the ultra-Orthodox family

Chapters 8 and 9 report the heart of the study: the differences or lack of differences that may be attributed to generation and to sex role within the ultra-Orthodox Jewish and the urban Arab communities. Our expectations are that in both communities the differences between sons and fathers will be greater than those between mothers and daughters. But in the Arab community, the reason for the differences between fathers and sons is that the sons are moving away from the traditional society and toward the larger society. The daughters, on the other hand, like their mothers are more committed to the traditional culture and life style. Both of them have fewer contacts with the larger society.

Among the ultra-Orthodox Jews the differences between fathers and sons are a function of the greater emphasis on orthodoxy and isolation from the larger society that the sons demand, compared with the fathers. The smaller differences between mothers and daughters are a function of the greater interest in and lesser insulation from the larger society that both of them share.

The overall results, we believe, will indicate that there are prospects for significant changes among the urban Arab population and that the direction of the changes is toward greater involvement and identification with the dominant culture and the larger society. Such a prospect will, if borne out, certainly be viewed as a mixed blessing by Jewish Israelis and as a distinct threat to the "Jewishness" of Israeli society.

The anticipated results for the ultra-Orthodox Jews are that the younger male members of that community are even more committed to segregation and insulation from the larger society than are their fathers, many of whom had to learn the techniques of compromise in order to survive individually and as a community in the Diaspora. For the ultra-Orthodox Jewish girls, the expected results suggest a greater interest in the larger society than their mothers had or their brothers have, but at the same time a deep commitment to the values associated with the role

132

of the traditional Jewish wife and mother. The two sets of desires are in conflict. We believe that the latter will take precedence over the former, with the result that the girls will not seek to break away from their community or become a source of tension or conflict within it.

The data will be presented as follows: For each sex role we shall compare the proportion of "agreement" within the same family. The unit of analysis in this and the next chapter is the dyad. We shall thus shift from the individual to the father and the son, and to the mother and the daughter. Where there is a great deal of consensus (say, more than two-thirds), we shall not detail the sources of the disagreement. But we shall provide more detail where the disagreement represents a larger proportion.

Fathers and sons

The first part compares the father-son dyad on matters that each engages in separately in order to see how similarly fathers and sons respond to issues such as voting preferences, mass media exposure, language usage, and leisure- or free-time activities. The second part reports the extent to which there is agreement or disagreement within the dyad about the son's behavior, interests, and plans for the future.

On language usage we asked three questions: What language do you speak at home? What language do you use at school or at work? Do you use any other language on other occasions? (And if so, what language and under what circumstances?) Fathers and sons agreed that at home they speak Yiddish. But then the consensus dropped considerably. At the yeshivas that most of the sons attend, the language is most often Yiddish. At work, about as many fathers employ Yiddish as Hebrew. In their responses to the last language usage item, the fathers demonstrated that they are more cosmopolitan than their sons. The latter are limited essentially to Yiddish and Hebrew, but the fathers draw upon their knowledge of Arabic, English, and several European languages such as Hungarian, Polish, Russian, and German.

The differences in amount and types of exposure to the mass media are consistent with the findings on language usage. Forty-seven percent of the dyads agree concerning their newspaper-reading habits. Sixty-six percent do not read any newspaper. But in those dyads in which there is disagreement (see Table 8.1), it is the sons much more than the fathers who do *not* read any newspaper. The fathers read the Agudat

Table 8.1. *Percentages of agreement and disagreement between fathers and sons about reading newspapers*

Read newspapers	Fathers and sons agree	Fathers and sons disagree	
		Sons' responses	Fathers' responses
No	31	42	4
Hamodia	9	2	22
Shearim	1	1	14
Hebrew secular	5	3	8
Hebrew religious	—	—	3
Yiddish	1	3	—
Other	—	1	2
No answer	—	1	—
Total	47	53	53

Party paper, *Hamodia,* and the Agudat Workers' Party paper, *Shearim.* Radio listening followed the newspaper pattern. Forty-seven percent of the dyads were in agreement. In the large majority of instances the agreement reflected that they do not listen to the radio because it is forbidden to do so. Among those dyads in which there was disagreement, most of the fathers said that they listen to the radio and most of the sons said they do not. Television viewing, however, was a different matter. On that issue there was consensus among 90 percent of the dyads: practically no one said they watched television.

Exposure to the mass media and language usage among the fathers and the sons revealed a consistent pattern. The sons maintain greater aloofness and insulation from the larger society than do the fathers. That same pattern appears when voting behaviors are compared. As shown in Table 8.2, when there is disagreement between fathers and sons, it is the sons who are more withdrawn and who maintain greater distance from the larger culture.

Sixty percent of the dyads agree, and in about half of them, the agreement is that neither the fathers nor the sons have voted nor plan to vote in the national elections. But among those 40 percent in which there is disagreement, it is because a higher proportion of the fathers claim that they do vote. In those families in which there was disagreement, the sons said that their failure to vote was not a function of

Table 8.2. *Percentages of agreement and disagreement between fathers and sons about voting in national elections*

		Fathers and sons disagree	
Voting preferences	Fathers and sons agree	Sons' responses	Fathers' responses
Do not/will not vote	27	29	11
Agudat Party	29	4	9
Other religious parties	1	4	3
Labor Alignment	–	–	1
Other	–	–	–
Refuse to reveal party	3	3	16
Total	60	40	40

apathy or indifference to national affairs, but a declaration of their resistance to recognizing the legitimacy of the state.

Both the fathers and sons were asked how they spend their time when they are not working or studying at the yeshiva. Phrasing such a question in this society is particularly complicated because there is no such concept as "spare" time. All of one's time that is not needed for work and the care of one's family should be devoted to the study of religious, sacred books. The legitimacy of "leisure" that is unrelated to the study of the Torah or to observing the Sabbath is not part of the culture of this society. The fact also that practically all of the sons (92 percent) attend yeshivas in which they engage in study, discussion, and prayer for ten hours or so a day detracts from the meaningfulness of the responses. Thus, as might have been anticipated, 61 percent of the dyads agreed that they spend their "free" time in prayer and religious service, and another 20 percent agreed that they spend their free time with their families. The 19 percent disagreement is explained by those boys who said they spend time with friends and in reading, whereas their fathers said they spend such time with their families.

Both the fathers and the sons were asked about the sons' current work and educational status and about plans for the sons' future. Practically all of the dyads (97 percent) answered the factual items in the same manner, thereby providing a check on the reliability of the responses, and also lending greater validity to their responses about the hopes and plans each has for the son's future. At the time of the survey,

92 percent of the sons were attending yeshivas. The other 8 percent were working.

Seventy-three percent of the dyads were in agreement about the sons' future education: They would continue to study at the yeshiva either until they were married or for the rest of their lives. If financial circumstances did not allow them to continue studying after they were married, they would find jobs that were related to or connected with their religious studies. In those families in which the fathers and sons disagreed about the son's future education, in practically all instances it was the fathers who expressed interest in having their sons study the sciences or the humanities and perhaps attend a university. With only one or two exceptions, none of the sons expressed interest in or desire to expand his learning beyond religious studies.

On another matter of importance to the sons' future, their marriage plans, most of the fathers and sons also saw eye to eye. Twenty-five percent of the sons were engaged to be married at the time of the survey. None of them had selected their bride-to-be alone; all of them had relied upon their parents or their parents and a professional matchmaker. Among those families in which the sons were not engaged, 43 percent of the dyads agreed on how the matter would be handled. Eight percent said that the son alone would select his bride; the others said that the parents and the matchmaker would initiate and handle the arrangements. Among those dyads in which there were disagreements, almost all of the disagreement centered on whether the sons' consent would be required before the parents and matchmaker made the final arrangements. Only 9 percent of the sons said that they expected to make their own marital arrangements.

Military service has been a fact of life for young people in Israel since the establishment of the state. Upon completion of high school or upon attaining the age of eighteen, young Jewish men and women are expected to serve in the army for three and two years respectively. As we learned earlier, there is one class of Jewish youth that is systematically excused: those boys who attend the yeshivas and those girls who claim that they are religious. The boys in the yeshivas are not deferred until after they have completed their studies; rather, they are exempted. In other words, they are not required to serve at any time. When a bill granting exemption from military service for yeshiva students was debated in the Israeli Parliament, it aroused more resentment and bitterness than almost any other proposal. Years later, it is still a source of resentment and disagreement within the society. Many youth who attend yeshivas in place of secondary schools enter the army upon completion of their course of study just as any other group of young Israeli men do. It is the young men within this ultra-Orthodox community who continue to study in the yeshiva past the age of eighteen, and toward whom the exemption status has been directed, who are the exceptions.

As shown by the response distribution in Table 8.3, most of the dyads are in agreement that the son will not serve in the army. But the explanation in the table footnote is of interest. It is another confirmation, along with the voting behavior and the mass media exposure, of the sons' greater adherence to isolation and separation from the larger society, and of their stronger commitment to the ultra-Orthodox community with its abhorrence of the secular Israeli way of life.

Table 8.3. *Percentages of agreement and disagreement between fathers and sons concerning their expectations about military service*

Expectations and beliefs about son's serving in army	Fathers and sons agree	Fathers and sons disagree	
		Sons' responses	Fathers' responses
Expect and believe son should serve	13	—	10
Father favors service, son opposes	—	—	—
Son favors service, father opposes	—	—	—
Neither expects son will serve	63[a]	16	—
No answer	5	3	9
Total	81	19	19

[a] Among these 63 percent, over 80 percent of the sons said they do not expect to serve because they are opposed to the state, and refusal to serve in its army is one of the most significant ways that they can declare their opposition to and separation from the larger society. Practically all of the fathers within this category, however, simply answered that their sons were yeshiva students, expected to remain students at the yeshiva and were, therefore, automatically exempted from military service. They did not use the occasion to declare their separation from and opposition to the state.

Both the fathers and the sons were asked whether they perceive disagreement and conflict with each other over the following topics: how the son spends his time, his choice of friends, his political interests, his style of dress, and his job. On each of these topics, save for the first, there was at least 90 percent agreement among the dyads, and the agreement was always such that the fathers approved of the sons' activities or ideas and that the sons perceived their fathers' approval of their behavior.

Even on the first topic, that of how the sons spend their time, the dyads agreed 60 percent of the time and the agreement was always in the direction of approval. In those families in which the fathers and sons disagreed it was most often because the sons perceived that the fathers disapproved of how they spent their time (e.g., they were lazy, they spent their time on frivolous activities) than that the fathers actually expressed disapproval. For example, 89 percent of the fathers said they approved of how their sons spend their time; but only 69 percent of the sons perceived their fathers' approval.

The final part of both the fathers' and the sons' interviews focused on the son's future in matters such as his financial circumstances, his ties to the community, how he will rear his children, whether he will continue with his studies, and how observant he will be of religious matters. Both the fathers and the sons perceive the future as being more differentiated and more complex than the present. There is the least consensus about the sons' future financial circumstances: Only 6 percent of the dyads in Table 8.4 are in agreement on this issue. The major sources of the disagreement stem either from the sons' beliefs that their circumstances will be essentially the same as their fathers', whereas the fathers believe that their sons will be better off than they are, or from differences about whether it is possible or sensible to make predictions about such matters. Those fathers who expect their sons to be better off than they are base their expectations on the fact that their sons are, or will be, better educated than they are and that there are more jobs available. The sons' beliefs are based on the simplistic idea that they plan to live their lives as their fathers have and therefore their fathers' financial circumstances must be a mirror of what their own will be.

On the matter of ties to the community, the sons are somewhat more likely than the fathers to see differences in their life styles. As the percentages in Table 8.5 indicate, 41 percent of the dyads perceive the

Table 8.4. *Percentages of agreement and disagreement between fathers and sons about sons' future financial circumstances*

Sons' future financial circumstances	Fathers and sons agree	Fathers and sons disagree	
		Sons' responses	Fathers' responses
Same as father	3	86	28
Sons better off than fathers	3	4	33
Sons less well off than fathers	–	–	3
Cannot predict	–	2	29
No answer	–	2	1
Total	6	94	94

Table 8.5. *Percentages of agreement and disagreement between fathers and sons about sons' ties to the community*

Sons' ties to the ultra-Orthodox community	Fathers and sons agree	Fathers and sons disagree	
		Sons' responses	Fathers' responses
Same as father	35	16	37
Father – stronger ties	1	4	4
Son – stronger ties	4	9	7
Father – secular ties, Son – religious ties	–	9	–
Different types of ties	–	19	3
Cannot predict	–	–	5
No answer	1	2	3
Total	41	59	59

future in the same way; but among the 59 percent who disagree it is the sons who are more likely to see divergence than the fathers. The direction of the divergence is not clear. The responses suggest that the major difference is that sons expect to be more active in religious organizations than their fathers.

Similarly, on the rearing of children, about half of the dyads expect no difference between the manner in which the fathers reared their children and the style in which the sons will rear theirs. But, as shown in Table 8.6, among those dyads in which there are disagreements, almost all of the sons perceive divergence in contrast to the fathers, almost all of whom anticipate continuity. Note that the sons emphasize one area of difference more than any other. They expect to be more permissive with their children than their fathers were with them.

Two-thirds of the dyads agreed on their perception of how the sons will spend their time when they are adults and on the degree of their religious observance. On both issues, the fathers and sons believed that the sons will follow in the fathers' footsteps. Among the one-third whose perceptions do not match, there is no consistent pattern.

Sixty-eight percent of the dyads also perceive the sons' education in the same manner: Forty-two percent believe that the sons will have as much of the same type of education as the fathers, and 26 percent believe that the sons will have more education, but of the same type as the fathers. Among the 32 percent who disagree, it is the fathers more than the sons who expect their sons to have more education than they did, but essentially of the same type.

In summary, in looking toward the future, most of the fathers and sons perceive continuity and similarity between themselves and their

Table 8.6. *Percentages of agreement and disagreement between fathers and sons about sons' rearing of children*

Rearing of sons' children	Fathers and sons agree	Fathers and sons disagree	
		Sons' responses	Fathers' responses
Same style	52	4	34
Son – would emphasize different values	–	1	1
Son – more permissive than father	1	30	2
Son – more strict than father	–	8	–
Son – more time with children	–	2	–
Other pattern	–	–	2
Cannot predict	–	–	8
No answer	–	2	–
Total	53	47	47

sons or fathers. The fathers are more optimistic about their sons' financial circumstances than are the sons, and the sons expect to rear their children more permissively than they themselves were reared, and to have more and different kinds of ties to their community than they perceive their fathers as having.

A review of all the father-son responses reveals that the sons are even more committed than the fathers toward a segregated and insulated life style and are more outspoken in their rejection of the dominant culture. Perhaps one important reason for the fathers' behavior is that they were born either in the Diaspora, where Jews had to live in an alien and often hostile society, or have vivid memories of ghetto life because of tales their fathers told them. Perhaps historical experiences such as these have made the fathers more flexible and more willing to compromise and to make some adjustments vis-à-vis the larger society, which is, after all, Jewish, albeit secular and nationalistic.

For their sons, such experiences are both less direct and more distant. Most of the boys have not personally been faced with the problem of learning how to survive in an alien culture while still managing to maintain their own identity. In a sense, the sons have the best of both worlds. On the one hand, the larger Israeli society provides a kind of cocoon, a protective coating in which they are able to express their beliefs and ideology in their purest forms and enjoy a life style that is most compatible with their religious values. On the other hand, that same society, toward which they feel superior, hostile, and different, excuses them from army service, from registering with government agencies, and from other demands that it places on its other adult Jewish citizens. It also protects their civil rights and religious observances. For example, automobiles are forbidden to pass through the streets of Mea Shearim on the Sabbath. There are thus few pressures either from within the community or from the larger society for changing, adjusting, or compromising. In the absence of such pressures, the sons do not show any significant signs that they are willing or inclined toward making changes on their own.

Mothers and daughters

In contrast to the father-son dyads, we anticipated smaller differences between the mothers and daughters because their sex roles offer them fewer opportunities for isolation from the larger society than do the male roles, and because the institutional structure of the ultra-Orthodox community dedicates itself more to preserving the sons' insulation than the daughters'. For example, it is the sons who are expected to remain in the yeshivas from early childhood until marriage and, ideally, all of their lives.

The daughters have more time to wander about, and in their wanderings they may more easily find themselves in contact with the larger society. A ten-minute bus ride, for example, takes them from the eighteenth- and nineteenth-century setting of Mea Shearim to the twentieth-century, cosmopolitan, worldly setting of Ben Yehuda Street and Jaffa Road, with their coffeehouses, boutiques, movie theaters, and so on. For these reasons alone, the women in this community, mothers as well as daughters, may be more worldly and more open to change than are the fathers and sons.

In reviewing the female responses in dyad form, we found that on the matter of language usage at home, 56 percent of the dyads are in agreement. Unlike the male respondents, both the mothers and the daughters claim that they speak Hebrew along with Yiddish. Given the prohibitions that exist against the use of Hebrew as a language for daily use, it is likely that the women speak Hebrew among themselves. When the mothers converse with their husbands and sons, or the daughters with their fathers and brothers, they probably speak Yiddish. Outside the home, both mothers and daughters use Hebrew and other European languages more than they do Yiddish.

The newspaper-reading habits of the female dyads, compared with those for the male dyads, also demonstrate the lesser isolation of the women. Although there is only 34 percent agreement between mothers and daughters concerning their reading habits, as Table 8.7 indicates, the disagreements focus on which types of newspapers they read, rather than on whether they read any at all. Among the dyads that manifest agreement, about one-third do not read any newspapers at all. As many of the daughters read newspapers other than those that represent the views of Agudat Party (or the Agudat Workers' Party), including the secular press, as limit their reading to "acceptable papers." At least one-third of the mothers read newspapers printed in Hungarian and German as well as from among the Hebrew secular press.

The same pattern is reflected in their responses to radio listening. Only a third of the dyads agree; but the disagreement centers on the number of hours they listen as opposed to whether they listen at all.

Table 8.7. *Percentages of agreement and disagreement between mothers and daughters about reading newspapers*

		Mothers and daughters disagree	
Read newspapers	Mothers and daughters agree	Daughters' responses	Mothers' responses
No	12	18	14
Hamodia	10	10	16
Shearim	2	10	–
Hebrew secular	4	12	8
Hebrew religious	6	14	4
Yiddish	–	2	4
Other (European language)	–	–	20
Total	34	66	66

Only 6 percent of the daughters, compared with 22 percent of the mothers, said they do not listen to the radio because it is forbidden. But in fact most of the mothers and the daughters said that they listen to the radio for several hours a day. When they were asked about the types of programs they listen to, most of the dyads agreed that they listen to all types: news, music, and stories.

Television viewing, however, was another matter. There was 62 percent agreement among the dyads on that issue, and among those who agreed, 85 percent said they never watch television. Fourteen percent of the mothers and 10 percent of the daughters acknowledge watching television occasionally, but none of them in their own homes!

Both the mothers' and the daughters' exposure to the mass media is greater than that of the fathers or the sons. Although the summarizing statistics do not demonstrate greater consensus among mothers and daughters, closer examination reveals that the differences are of degree rather than of kind.

The responses to the questions about voting behavior make the same point. Fifty-six percent of the female dyads agree (in contrast to 60 percent of the males), and the agreement is in the direction that they vote or plan to vote for the Agudat Party. But many more of the sons as opposed to the fathers, 56 percent versus 38 percent (see Table 8.2), do not plan to vote at all, as opposed to the daughters and mothers,

Table 8.8. *Percentages of agreement and disagreement between mothers and daughters about voting in national elections*

Vote in national elections	Mothers and daughters agree	Mothers and daughters disagree	
		Daughters' responses	Mothers' responses
Do not/will not vote	6	18	26
Agudat Party	48	14	8
Other religious parties	2	4	2
Labor Alignment	–	2	–
Other	–	4	2
Refuse to reveal party	–	2	6
Total	56	44	44

where the difference is 24 percent versus 32 percent (see Table 8.8).

In this next portion, the emphasis shifts to an examination of the mothers' and daughters' perceptions and opinions about the daughters' behavior and life circumstances. About 65 percent of the daughters were attending school at the time of the survey (in contrast to 92 percent of the sons).[1] Those who had stopped going to school had done so because they finished their course of study or because they were needed at home to help with the younger children.

Seventy-two percent of the dyads are in agreement about the kind of work the daughter is likely to do when she finishes school. Teaching was by far the most popular choice. Only 6 percent of the mothers and none of the daughters said that they planned to have the daughters remain at home and not work when they finish school, or that the daughters were at home and not working if they had already completed school. The pattern then is for the young girls to work outside their homes as teachers before they are married, a pattern that has clearly not been established for their brothers.

Twelve percent of the daughters were engaged to be married at the time of the survey. In five out of the six cases, the bridegroom was a yeshiva student. There was 42 percent agreement among the dyads as to how the husbands ought to be selected for those not engaged. The most dominant pattern is for the parents and matchmaker to initiate the arrangements and then seek the girl's consent. But note that where there is disagreement among the dyads in Table 8.9 it is the mothers

Table 8.9. *Percentages of agreement and disagreement between mothers and daughters about selection of husbands for daughters*

		Mothers and daughters disagree	
Selection of husbands	Mothers and daughters agree	Daughters' responses	Mothers' responses
Parents and matchmaker	10	32	24
Parents, matchmaker – with daughters' consent	18	16	18
Daughters	8	2	12
No answer	6	8	4
Total	42	58	58

who are more likely than the daughters to expect the girl and boy to seek each other out and make their own marital arrangements.

Among the fathers and sons, there was a higher proportioin of agreement that the parents and matchmakers would make the arrangements, and in those instances in which there was disagreement it was because some of the sons disagreed with their fathers and said they planned to initiate their own marital arrangements. But, on the whole, a higher proportion of the male dyads expected that the parent, with the assistance of the matchmaker, would make all the necessary arrangements.

A similar pattern, whereby the mothers are more open and more willing to divert somewhat from the traditional paths, may be seen in the distribution of responses (described in Table 8.10) to the question of how many children the mothers and daughters expect the daughters to have. Most of the 44 percent agreement among the dyads stemmed from those who said one cannot, and should not try, to predict such matters. Among those dyads in which there was disagreement, it was the daughters who were more likely to say "the same number of children as my mother" or "more."

In that portion of the interview in which the mothers and daughters were both asked how each of them perceived the daughter's choice of friends, how the daughter spends her time, her style of dress, whether she will be as observant of the rituals as her mother, and more generally whether she will lead the kind of life that her mother does, there was at least 78 percent agreement. The shared perceptions of the daughters' actual and expected behaviors also indicated approval on the part of the

Table 8.10. *Percentages of agreement and disagreement between mothers and daughters about number of children daughter is likely to have*

		Mothers and daughters disagree	
Number of children	Mothers and daughters agree	Daughters' responses	Mothers' responses
Same number as mother	4	22	4
Fewer than mother	–	10	–
More than mother	2	8	4
What God gives	2	12	28
Cannot predict	36	–	10
Whatever daughter wants	–	4	10
Total	44	56	56

mothers and perceived approval by the daughters. For example, on the matter of observing the rituals, 91 percent of the dyads said that the daughters will observe them as their mothers do; and in general on the kind of life the daughters will lead as adults, over 86 percent of the dyads said that the daughters will conduct their lives as their mothers do.

In the final part of the interview that focused on the daughter's future, there were several topics about which the proportion of dyads who saw eye to eye was relatively low and about which daughters expressed inclinations that were different from those of their mothers. An example is the issue of whether the daughters would work outside the home after they are married. As the distribution in Table 8.11 shows, among the dyads that expressed consensus and among those that did not, the prevailing pattern is that although the mothers remained at home after they were married, the daughters expect to work.

On the matter of the kinds of interests the daughters are likely to have after they are married, compared with those of the mothers, one-third of the dyads expected the daughters' interests to match those of the mothers (which are their home and child rearing). About one-third of the daughters disagreed with their mothers and expected their interests would diverge somewhat; the daughters believed that they would be more interested in reading and other intellectual pursuits. The other third declined to predict what their interests after marriage would be.

Table 8.11. *Percentages of agreement and disagreement between mothers and daughters about whether daughters will work outside the home after marriage*

Will daughter work outside home?	Mothers and daughters agree	Mothers and daughters disagree	
		Daughters' responses	Mothers' responses
Yes, but mother does not	30	28	10
Both will work after children are grown	6	4	2
Neither will work — nor expects to	14	8	8
Other pattern	—	10	10
Don't know	—	—	20
Total	50	50	50

Fifty-six percent of the dyads agreed on how the daughters would dress (over 80 percent said that they would dress as their mothers do); but among those who disagreed, about half of the daughters thought their style would be more modern than that of their mothers, whereas more of the mothers thought their daughters would follow in their footsteps.

On the issues of how the daughters would relate to their husbands, and how they would rear their children, 70 percent and 68 percent of the dyads concurred. The dominant pattern on both issues was that the daughter and husband would decide matters jointly, as they perceive their mothers and fathers do, and that their children would be reared as they have been. There was no greater tendency for the daughters, as opposed to the mothers, to perceive themselves as diverging from the traditional patterns.

On the matter of how observant of religion in general the daughters were expected to be, 74 percent of the dyads agreed that the daughters would be as observant as the mothers and the mothers were perceived to be observant of the traditions.

In conclusion, the findings in this chapter provide some evidence for the expectation that the women in the ultra-Orthodox community are more likely to be agents of social change than are the men. The women (younger and older) are more interested in and more involved in the affairs of the larger society than are the men, as indicated by their responses to the questions about mass media, language usage, and voting. Unlike the pattern observed among the fathers and sons, we found no evidence that the daughters were more resistant to change, more insistent on tradition, more isolated, and more anxious to remain insulated from the larger society than their mothers.

On the other hand, we found neither wide differences between mothers and daughters nor any strong indications that the younger generation was on the brink of revolting from traditional ways. Given the subservient position that women occupy in the ultra-Orthodox community, their interest and willingness to involve themselves in the larger society will have to become considerably stronger before they are able to make much of an impact on their community. The next generation of young women are most likely to continue a mild flirtation in a "peek-a-boo" style with the larger society while still retaining a basically traditional, ultra-Orthodox life style. Finally, the winds of social change may be felt in their mildest form across the ultra-Orthodox community. But for the next generation, the prospect of continuity, insulation, and rejection of contacts with the larger society appears to be the order of the day.

9. Sex and generational roles in the urban Arab family

This chapter follows the pattern established in chapter 8. Our anticipations about the Israeli Arabs were that there would be differences in perspectives, life styles, and ambitions between the parents' and children's generations, and that among the younger generation, the boys especially would be likely to have their eyes, and many of their thoughts, directed at the larger, Jewish Israeli society rather than toward their parents and their more traditional Arab society.

In part, we expected that the parents would be supportive of their children's aspiration for closer contacts with the larger society and for the educational and occupational opportunities that are likely to result from such contacts. But we also anticipated that the parents would be fearful that with more extensive contacts would come acculturation and perhaps rejection of their own society. Of course, both the parents and children are likely to recognize that the door to the larger society is not standing open to them. No invitations are being issued for them to enter into the business, social, and political life of the larger society.

Although there are obvious barriers at the security-related institutions, it is still possible for Arabs to enter many of the institutions of the larger society and find opportunities available within them. Thus, although limited, the younger urban Arab generation has some choices about how much it wishes to participate in and become involved with the Jewish Israeli society.

Fathers and sons

The distribution of responses about language usage shows that the sons have greater opportunities to use Hebrew than do their fathers. Although at home practically all of the dyads report that Arabic is spoken exclusively (92 percent), at work and at school there is 70 percent disagreement on language usage. As the percentages in Table 9.1 show, the major difference between the fathers and sons arises from the higher

149

proportion of sons who use Hebrew exclusively. When asked about their language usage on other occasions, there was 36 percent agreement among the dyads. The disagreement is largely a result of a higher proportion of the fathers who do not speak any language except Arabic (33 percent vs. 18 percent) and a higher proportion of the sons who speak Hebrew.

The fathers' and sons' exposure to the mass media also revealed a pattern whereby the sons have greater contacts with the larger society, as shown by the distribution of responses in Table 9.2. Thirty-four percent of the sons read a Hebrew- and/or European-language news-

Table 9.1. *Percentages of agreement and disagreement between fathers and sons about languages spoken at work or school*

		Fathers and sons disagree	
Language at work or school	Fathers and sons agree	Sons's responses	Fathers' responses
Arabic	7.3	22.4	24.8
Hebrew	14.5	32.8	16.8
Arabic and Hebrew	8.1	12.0	28.0
Arabic and English	—	1.6	—
Hebrew and English	—	0.8	—
Total	29.9	69.6	69.6

Table 9.2. *Percentages of agreement and disagreement between fathers and sons about reading newspapers*

		Fathers and sons disagree	
Read newspapers	Fathers and sons agree	Sons' responses	Fathers' responses
No	41.1	12.8	26.6
Hebrew press	2.4	28.0	2.4
Arabic press	0.8	5.6	16.6
Arabic and Hebrew/ European	3.2	6.4	7.2
Total	47.5	52.8	52.8

paper, compared with 10 percent of the fathers. It is surprising that 41 percent of the dyads claim they do not read any newspapers regularly. Some of the explanation for the fathers' responses is due to their lack of literacy; but illiteracy is not at all helpful in explaining the sons' behavior.

Only 6 percent of the respondents do not listen to the radio. What differentiates the fathers' from the sons' responses is that 40 percent of the sons, compared with 14 percent of the fathers, listen to the Hebrew-language programs regularly.

Seventy-five percent of the families have television sets. Unlike the radio-listening pattern, in which there was a clear difference between the fathers and the sons in their language preference, in the case of television viewing, both prefer programs in Arabic. The sons have only a slight edge over their fathers in the proportion that watch programs in Hebrew as well as in Arabic — 30 percent versus 20 percent. Watching programs in Arabic means programs that originate in Israel and also in Lebanon, Jordan, Egypt, and Syria, each of which is available to some Israelis, depending on the part of the country.

There were three questions that focused directly on political issues: voting behavior, military service for the sons, and how the fathers and the sons felt about the sons' interest in politics. In response to each of them, the sons were more guarded and less candid than their fathers. For example, on the voting question, as the distribution of percents in Table 9.3 shows, more of the sons were unwilling to say which party they supported than were the fathers (45 percent vs. 22 percent).

Note also, that practically all the respondents vote or expect to vote in the national elections. These responses are consistent with the percentage of Arabs voting in all of the prior Israeli elections. The substance of the responses is also consistent with those described in Chapter 3. The largest proportion of Arab voters support the party in power, the Labor Alignment. That has been the pattern since 1948. But the high proportion of sons who refused to say which party they support leads one to the surmise that fathers and sons disagree on this issue more than is revealed by the data in Table 9.3. It would be a reasonable guess that many of those sons vote or plan to vote the Rakah ticket, whereas their fathers continue to support the Labor Alignment.

The differences in responses that were revealed by the question about how the fathers and sons are most likely to spend their spare time when they are not at work or at school are the same as those that

Table 9.3. *Percentages of agreement and disagreement between fathers and sons about voting in national elections*

		Fathers and sons diagree	
Voting preferences	Fathers and sons agree	Sons' responses	Fathers' responses
Do not/will not vote	1.6	0.8	1.6
Labor Alignment	34.7	7.2	32.0
Rakah	0.8	2.4	2.4
Other	1.6	5.6	3.2
Refuse to reveal which party	13.7	31.2	8.0
Total	52.4	47.2	47.2

might have been found in many other societies. There is only a 19 percent overlap among the dyads, essentially because the sons prefer the company of their friends, and the fathers prefer to be with their families and at religious services.

This next section shifts the focus from those activities and interests that the fathers and sons might each pursue separately, to an examination of the responses that the fathers and sons gave to various aspects of their sons' life style and future behavior. According to the responses in the dyads, about 42 percent of the boys were still attending school at the time of the survey. Six more sons than fathers said that they were still in school. Over 70 percent of the dyads agreed about why the sons were no longer at school: because they had finished their course of study by completing either the eighth grade or the compulsory tenth grade. A few more fathers than sons (12 percent vs. 6 percent) said that the sons had stopped going to school because they had lost interest. A third of the dyads said that they expect that the sons will remain in school at least until they complete secondary school (the twelfth grade). Only three fathers and none of the sons said that they hoped that their sons would go on to a university.

When the fathers were asked whether they agreed with their sons' decisions about school and jobs, and when the sons were asked how they perceived their fathers' reactions to their plans and current behavior, 86 percent of the dyads perceived consensus or had not thought about the issues in question.

Table 9.4. *Percentages of agreement and disagreement between fathers and sons concerning their expectations about military service*

Expectations and beliefs about sons serving in army	Fathers and sons agree	Fathers and sons disagree	
		Sons' responses	Fathers' responses
Believe sons should serve	1.6	2.4	5.6
Arabs are not allowed to serve	63.7	29.6	4.0
Arabs are not allowed to serve and should not serve	–	2.4	24.8
Total	65.3	34.4	34.4

The same high level of consensus was manifest in the fathers' and sons' responses to the items about the sons' future marital plans. Only 5 percent of the boys were engaged at the time of the survey, so almost all of the answers are conjectures about the future. Nevertheless, when asked how the son's future wife was likely to be selected, 74 percent of the dyads agreed. Within that 74 percent, all but 2 percent said that the sons would select his own bride and make the necessary arrangements. Even among the remaining 26 percent of the dyads, there was no pattern that was determined by generation or role. Seventy-seven percent of the dyads anticipated no conflict or disagreement about the son's choice of a bride or the manner in which she would be selected.

Arab youth are exempt from military service. They may volunteer, and if upon investigation they are found acceptable, they may serve. But that happens rarely, and the predominant pattern is for Arab youth not to share in the all-important citizen-socializing experience in which the great majority of Jewish Israeli adolescents participate. When the fathers and sons were asked not only whether they expected their sons to serve in the army, but how they felt about their sons serving or not serving, 65 percent of the dyads agreed. For all but two families, the agreement was that the son should not serve. But note how the responses shown in Table 9.4 are distributed among the fathers and sons who did not agree.

About 25 percent of the fathers said that their sons cannot serve in the Israeli army because they are Arabs, and they do not believe that they should serve. Arabs, in whatever country they live are cousins, and they believe that they should not kill or harm each other. The sons, however, avoided expressing any opinion on the issue of their military service. They responded only by repeating that their formal status exempted them from military obligations. The sons' responses on this issue, as on their voting preferences, indicate less candor and less willingness to express an opinion than do their fathers'.

In that portion of the interview that asked the sons and fathers whether they shared opinions about how the son usually spent his time, about his choice of friends, his style of dress, his political interests, and his job, we found a high proportion of consensus on the last three issues and less agreement on the first two. As the distributions in Tables 9.5 and 9.6 indicate, 52 and 41 percent of the dyads do not agree on how the son spends his time and on his choice of friends. Seventy-two percent of the dyads are in agreement about how much and what type of political interests their sons have; 84 percent agreed on their sons' style of dress, and 77 percent agreed on the sons' choice of work.

But the fact that the fathers and sons by and large agree about the sons' current life circumstances turned out to be a poor predictor about how much consensus there was concerning the sons' behavior and life style as an adult. We found that when the fathers and sons were asked

Table 9.5. *Percentages of agreement and disagreement between fathers and sons concerning how sons spend their time*

		Fathers and sons disagree	
Perceptions on sons' use of time	Fathers and sons agree	Sons' responses	Fathers' responses
No disagreement	46.8	18.4	24.0
Son does not do enough/ wastes his time	–	7.2	20.8
Sons want to work/fathers think school more important	–	7.2	–
Father disagrees with son's political activities	–	7.2	–
Disagree – other reasons	–	13.0	8.0
Total	46.8	53.0	52.8

Table 9.6. *Percentages of agreement and disagreement between fathers and sons concerning sons' choice of friends*

Perceptions of sons' friends	Fathers and sons agree	Fathers and sons disagree	
		Sons' responses	Fathers' responses
Approve of friends	56.5	23.2	15.2
Disapprove of things friends do	2.4	8.0	25.6
Disapprove of friends — are not of comparable families	—	9.6	—
Total	58.9	40.8	40.8

how they thought they (or their sons) would rear their children, spend their time, observe their religion, and whether the sons would have a comparable education, similar financial circumstances, and ties to the community, only a minority of the dyads perceived the fathers' life as a model or a blueprint for the sons. On most issues, both the fathers and the sons expected the sons to lead different kinds of lives than their fathers did.

As the distributions in Table 9.7 through 9.10 demonstrate, less than a third of the dyads perceived the fathers' life as a model for the sons. Only on the matter of religious observance did a majority of both sons and fathers (although not in the same families) believe that the sons would be as observant as their fathers (see Table 9.7). (In most instances "as observant" meant not particularly observant of religious practices and prayers.)

Table 9.8 shows that 70 percent of the fathers, compared with 49 percent of the sons (and only a third of the dyads), expected that the sons would spend their nonworking time as the fathers have. Most of the sons expect to spend less time in the coffeehouses and more time with their families. We commented in Chapter 5 that the sons were particularly critical of their fathers for the time they spend in the coffeehouses talking and playing cards.

Only on the matter of the sons' future financial circumstances did more of the sons than their fathers perceive similarity. Included in the category "same as fathers" in Table 9.9 are those dyads who believe that the fathers and their families enjoy comfortable circumstances as well as those who feel they do not.

Table 9.7. *Percentages of agreement and disagreement between fathers and sons about sons' religious observance in the future*

Sons' future religious observance	Fathers and sons agree	Fathers and sons disagree	
		Sons' responses	Fathers' responses
Same as fathers	8.9	52.4	47.0
Fathers more observant than sons	—	4.1	32.2
Sons more observant than fathers	1.6	13.8	5.1
Cannot predict	—	18.5	5.1
Total	10.5	88.8	89.4

Table 9.8. *Percentages of agreement and disagreement between fathers and sons about how sons will spend their time*

How sons spend time — future	Fathers and sons agree	Fathers and sons disagree	
		Sons' responses	Fathers' responses
Same	33.1	16.0	36.8
Father — coffeehouse; son — home	—	20.0	1.6
Father — home; son — community	—	—	12.8
Father — community; son — home	—	24.8	—
Other pattern	—	3.4	12.8
Cannot predict	—	2.6	2.4
Total	33.1	66.8	66.4

The topic on which more of the sons perceived differences with their fathers than any of the others concerned the rearing of children. Over 80 percent of the sons expect that they will behave differently toward their children. Most of them as Table 9.10 shows, believe that they will be more permissive than their fathers were toward them. For the fathers, this issue and perhaps the one on how they spend their time,

Table 9.9. *Percentages of agreement and disagreement between fathers and sons about sons' future financial circumstances*

Sons' future financial circumstances	Fathers and sons agree	Fathers and sons disagree	
		Sons' responses	Fathers' responses
Same as fathers	2.4	43.2	20.8
Sons better off than fathers	19.3	33.0	36.8
Sons less well off than fathers	—	—	4.0
Cannot predict	0.8	0.8	16.2
Total	22.5	77.0	77.8

Table 9.10. *Percentages of agreement and disagreement between fathers and sons about sons' rearing of children*

Rearing of sons' children	Fathers and sons agree	Fathers and sons disagree	
		Sons' responses	Fathers' responses
Same style	8.9	8.0	31.2
Son more permissive than father	7.3	58.0	1.6
Son more strict than father	—	5.6	—
Son emphasized different values	3.2	7.2	29.6
Other pattern	—	—	—
Cannot predict	—	2.4	17.6
Total	19.4	80.2	80.0

are more sensitive and more personal than the others in this section. On both, the fathers are much more likely to see the sons following in their footsteps or claiming that they cannot predict how their sons are likely to behave.

In summary, upon examination of all the data presented in dyad form, it appears that the original expectation about the sons having their eyes directed toward the larger community and away from the fathers' more traditional life style has been borne out. The younger generation does appear to be divesting itself of many of the prescribed modes of behavior characteristic of their fathers' society. There is evidence in the sons' language usage, in their contacts with the mass media, in their style of dress, in their marriage plans, in how they spend their time, and in their religious commitments, that the sons are adopting behaviors and ideas that are compatible with the dominant secular, Jewish Israeli life styles.

In most instances, the fathers have not assumed a position that places them in conflict with their sons. Rather, the fathers seem to perceive their sons' interests and emulation of the dominant culture as inevitable: They do not confront the sons with the choice of either living fully within the prescribed patterns of the Arab community or of making a complete break with that community. Perhaps because of the fathers' attitudes, the changes that are likely to occur among the younger male members of the Arab community will not result in a sharp rift between the older and younger generations and in a wholesale dismantling of the community within one or two generations. Perhaps, too, many of the distinctive characteristics of the Israeli Arab culture will continue to exist alongside a growing "Israelization" of that community. Behavior and beliefs that will continue to set them apart from the larger society will be primarily in the political sphere and in the day-to-day social contacts involving friendships, dating, marriage, and so on. The separateness that is reflected in these matters will be as much a reflection of the wishes of the larger society as it will be of the interests of the Arabs themselves.

Mothers and daughters

We anticipated that the differences between the mothers and daughters in the Arab community would be smaller than those between the fathers and sons, but that many of the daughters, like their brothers, would also have their faces turned toward the larger society. Many of the daughters already are showing signs of having adopted the characteristics and mannerisms of the young girls who compose the mainstream of Israeli society. These changes manifest themselves most clearly in the girls' interest in more schooling, in holding a job before they are married, in their style of dress, in how they say they will meet their future husband, and in the number of children they plan to have.

Traditionally in Arab society daughters have been more protected, more insulated, and more dependent than sons. Both the mothers and fathers are likely to be more reluctant to have their daughters exposed to the influences of the larger society than they are their sons; and the daughters are less likely to assert themselves at the cost of rejecting the influence and authority of their parents. But given the values and social organization of Arab society, the behavior and stance that the men assume vis-à-vis the dominant culture is likely to determine the relationship that both sexes eventually will have toward the larger society. Thus even if the attitudes of the young girls in this survey do not support the expectations described previously, we would nevertheless predict a movement toward emulation and adoption of the life styles of the larger Israeli society because within Arab culture it is the men who are more likely to determine the life styles of their families.

All of the mothers and daughters speak only Arabic at home. On other occasions, such as shopping or when they are with friends, there is only 12 percent agreement among the dyads, but that small proportion, it turns out, is completely accounted for by the fact that the daughters speak Hebrew, English, or some other language in addition to Arabic, and that 36 percent of the mothers do not know any other language except Arabic.

There is 42 percent agreement among the dyads about exposure to the mass media. Most of that agreement is a function of the fact that neither mother nor daughter reads a newspaper regularly. In total, 76 percent of the mothers, compared with 24 percent of the daughters, do not read any newspaper. Almost all of the mothers' behavior can probably be explained by their lack of schooling. Among the daughters who do read a newspaper regularly, about 80 percent limit their exposure to newspapers in Arabic, which may be a function of their literacy.

All of the dyads (save 2 percent) listen to the radio, and the great majority listen to all types of programs for many hours a day, but only in Arabic. Sixty-eight percent of the dyads own a television set. They watch programs exclusively in Arabic. Save, then, for the greater proportion of daughters who read newspapers (in Arabic), there are no major differences between mothers and daughters in their exposure to the mass media.

A majority of the dyads also responded in the same way to the question about voting in the national elections. Like the Arab men, practically all of the women reported that they vote (or plan to vote), and the Labor Alignment, the party in power, receives the support of most of them (see Table 9.11). The daughters' responses are similar to their brothers' in one important respect. Both of them, in contrast to either the mothers or the fathers, are more likely to refuse to name the party they support. We interpret the daughters' lack of response in the same way we did the sons'.

This next section examines the dyads' perceptions and attitudes about the daughters' behavior and their prospects for the future. Most of the girls (63 percent) were no longer attending school at the time of the survey. More than 75 percent had completed at least the tenth grade before stopping, but none had gone further than fourteen years. Most of the mothers and daughters agreed that the daughters who were no longer in school had completed their course of study. Ninety-eight percent of the dyads expressed consensus and approval at the daughters' course of action. Practically all of the girls who are working and those who are still in school said that they are now working or plan to work

Table 9.11. *Percentages of agreement and disagreement between mothers and daughters about voting in national elections*

Vote in national elections	Mothers and daughters agree	Mothers and daughters disagree	
		Daughters' responses	Mothers' responses
Do not/will not vote	2	–	2
Labor Alignment	24	10	26
Rakah	–	8	4
Other	–	4	4
Refuse to indicate party	26	26	12
Total	52	48	48

as teachers or in some other white-collar job; but teaching was the most popular choice.

Twelve percent of the girls were engaged at the time of the survey. Half of them had selected their husband without their parents' initial intervention. The prospective grooms work as skilled laborers. Fifty-two percent of the dyads in families in which the daughters were not engaged expressed consensus about how the future husband would be selected. Although the dominant pattern is for the young people to initiate their own arrangements, as the percentages in Table 9.12 show, the disagreements are also most likely to occur in those families in which the daughter expects to select a husband without her parents' intervention.

Sixty-four percent of the dyads agreed about how old the daughters were likely to be at the time of their marriage. The age selected by most of them was twenty-one (only 2 percent thought that the girl would be married before she was seventeen).

The dyads expressed a high degree of approval about the daughters' current life style and about their futures. There was at least 82 percent approval or agreement about how the daughters spend their time, their choice of friends, and their style of dress. Seventy and 76 percent, respectively, also anticipated that the mothers would approve of the daughters' religious observances and of the kind of life they would lead when they were adults.

Table 9.12. *Percentages of agreement and disagreement between mothers and daughters about selection of husbands for daughters*

		Mothers and daughters disagree	
Selection of husband	Mothers and daughters agree	Daughters' responses	Mothers' responses
Parents	22	6	8
Parents and matchmakers	–	14	16
Parents with daughters' consent	–	4	6
Girl and boy – alone	30	24	16
No answer	–	–	2
Total	52	48	48

Table 9.13. *Percentages of agreement and disagreement between mothers and daughters about number of children daughter is likely to have*

| | | Mothers and daughters disagree | |
Number of children	Mothers and daughters agree	Daughters' responses	Mothers' responses
Same number as mother	6	—	4
Fewer than mother	58	22	6
More than mother	10	4	2
Whatever daughter wants	—	—	10
Cannot predict	—	—	4
Total	74	26	26

But as we shall note in the data to be presented, the high level of approval does not mean that the mothers and daughters anticipated that the daughters' life style would match that of the mothers. For example, as the percentages in Table 9.13 show, 58 out of 74 percent of the dyads who expressed agreement about the number of children they thought the daughters would have agreed that the daughters would have fewer children than the mothers. Indeed, in total, 80 percent of the daughters said they expected to have fewer children than their mothers. But it should be noted that this was also the expectation of 64 percent of the mothers.

Along the same lines, we found that at least 60 percent of the dyads agreed about whether the daughters would work outside the home after they were married, how they would rear their children, how they would dress, and how observant they would be of religious practices; but in each instance, the agreement meant that both mothers and daughters anticipated that the daughters would behave differently than the mothers.[1] Sixty-six percent of the dyads expect the daughters to work outside their homes after they are married, although the mothers do not. Fifty-six percent of the dyads expect that the daughters will dress in a modern motif although the mothers do not. (This means the daughters will wear Western dress rather than the traditional garb of the Arab women.) Thirty percent of the dyads expect that the daughters will emphasize values in the rearing of their children that are different from their mothers'; and 42 percent expect that the daughters will be less observant of religious practices than the mothers.

Table 9.14. *Percentages of agreement and disagreement between mothers and daughters about daughters' interests and activities after marriage*

Daughters' interests and activities	Mothers and daughters agree	Mothers and daughters disagree	
		Daughters' responses	Mothers' responses
Same	12	12	24
Mother at home/daughter organizations	4	6	4
Mother at home/daughter movies, restaurants	12	38	6
Mother at home/daughter intellectual (reading, lectures, etc.)	2	14	36
Total	30	70	70

Mothers and daughters also agreed that the daughters will have interests that are different from those of the mothers, but they disagree about what the daughters' interests are likely to be. As shown in Table 9.14, the biggest difference that the mothers perceive between themselves and their daughters is that their daughters will be more interested in intellectual matters than they are. But the daughters see things somewhat differently. They expect that they will be more interested in going to movies, restaurants, and other places of entertainment, places to which Arab husbands usually go — but not accompanied by their wives.

To conclude, these data have shown that changes are occurring among the younger generation of urban Arab women and that the changes are in the direction of the adoption of the life styles and ways of thinking of the larger culture. Although the young girls today may still be living in a traditional Arab society, both they and their mothers expect that they will adopt many of the characteristics of the Jewish Israeli society when they move into their own family units. Among the most significant of the changes that both the mothers and the daughters anticipate is that the daughters will select their own husbands, will have fewer children, and will work as clerks and teachers after they are married.

The findings reported earlier concerning the sons' expectations about their futures suggest that the types of adaptions the girls anticipate making in their own roles will be compatible with the interests and changes planned by the young men.

10. Summary and conclusions: a look at the future

The conclusions that may be drawn from this survey are clear and straightforward and can be stated briefly. The adolescents in the ultra-Orthodox Jewish community show hardly any of the signs of revolt or strain or disenchantment with their parents' culture and life style that characterize the moods and behavior of adolescents in many other societies throughout the world. What these results demonstrate most clearly is the strength and the cohesion that exist within the ultra-Orthodox community and the absence of strain between the generations. On the basis of the data collected, and assuming no catastrophic external interference, we would predict that if a survey was to be conducted twenty years hence in Mea Shearim, the attitudes and attachments of that generation of adolescents would be basically unchanged from those reported in 1971.

With practically no exceptions, members of the older generation of respondents believe that their lives are special, that their culture and their values are superior to those held and practiced by the rest of Israeli society, and indeed to most of the rest of the world, and that their beliefs and practices will survive long after those of most of the contemporary world have ceased to exist.

As far as we can tell, to a very large extent the parents and other representative adults of this community have successfully transmitted this sense of specialness and superiority to their youth. The adolescents, especially the boys, are committed to their parents' and to their grandparents' beliefs and to a life devoted to the study of sacred books (the Torah and the Talmud) and to prayer. To the young girls, the most desirable husband is one who has demonstrated that he has talent in these matters.

Both the older and younger generations are extremely selective about which part of the larger culture they allow themselves to come in contact with: Schools, television, the army, and places of entertainment are taboo; but newspapers, radio, and political institutions (such as the voting booth) are acceptable within specified limits.

164

On issues that affect the younger generation most directly — marriage, children, education, jobs — we found little indication that the adolescent respondents desired or planned to arrange their lives differently from the way they believe their parents expected them to live. A minority of the girls expect to have more schooling and wider interests than their mothers, and perhaps more comfortable and easier life circumstances. But even among this small group, most of the girls expect that their parents will arrange their marriage for them, and that they will have as many children as their mothers had.

For the boys, there was even less evidence that they were, or would be, diverting from the path of ultra-Orthodoxy. The army, secular education, and success in the occupational or professional worlds appear to be neither in their immediate future nor in their dreams. The immediateness and the accessibility of the larger culture make it no more likely that this generation of ultra-Orthodox youth will cross the threshold than it was when the gates of the ghettos in which their grandfathers lived were locked with iron bars every night.

Among the urban Arab community the story is quite different, however. Here we found people of two generations, parents and adolescents, who, on the one hand, recognize that changes in their life styles are inevitable and, on the other, seem to welcome them and wish to extend themselves to meet many of those changes.

We did not find that the parents themselves were changing their life styles so as to adapt to the larger society. In large measure, the parents appear to be remaining loyal to their traditional practices, be it in the manner of dress, in how they spend their leisure, in their use of language, and in their contacts with the mass media. But at the same time that their own lives are remaining relatively unchanged, they are accepting of, and positive in their attitudes toward, the larger culture, as represented, for example, in their responses to the questions about child-rearing practices, sexual behavior, and education in the larger society. There was none of the sense of superiority and exclusiveness that so characterized the stance of the ultra-Orthodox community vis-à-vis the larger society.

Nor did the parents appear to be in conflict with their children's desires to take on many of the characteristics of the larger culture. The mothers, for example, anticipated that their daughters would select their own husbands, would work outside their homes after they were married, would discard traditional Arab garb for Western dress, would have fewer children, would have interests in matters about which the mothers were ignorant, and would be less observant of religious practices. The daughters also would be more likely to go with their husbands to movies, cafés, lectures, that is, to places where husbands traditionally went with other men. They would be more likely to vote and to participate in community affairs.

The sons, even more than the daughters, seemed to be desirous of moving into the larger society and taking on many of the characteristics of that society. In so doing, they also revealed negative attitudes toward their fathers' way of life. The targets most often attacked by the sons were the fathers' lack of success in the occupational world and their failure to provide adequately for their families. They seemed to attribute part of this failure to the fathers' propensity to spend long periods of time in the coffeehouses talking and playing cards with their friends. The coffeehouses not only interfered with time that the fathers could have used for earning a better living, but they also interfered with time that could have been spent with their families. The sons criticize their fathers for not spending enough time with their children, for having more children than they are able to care for, and for not showing enough interest in and attention to the children they have. In discussing their own futures, the sons emphasized that they would have smaller families to whom they would be more devoted, and that they would spend more time with their children.

Both the fathers and the sons expected that the sons' financial circumstances will be better than those of the fathers. The fact that most of the sons will have had more years of schooling than their fathers could by itself explain the expectation of improved financial circumstances, even if a stronger work ethic was not also involved. As adolescents, the sons already seem to have more contacts with and interest in the larger society than do the fathers, as represented by the higher proportion of sons who use Hebrew regularly and who read the Hebrew press.

One topic about which fathers and sons agreed, and which reflects a desire on both their parts to remain aloof from the larger culture, concerned the sons' army service. Neither the fathers nor the sons expected the sons to serve in the Israeli army. About a quarter of the sons were more direct in their responses about not wanting to serve than were the fathers, but in essence both agreed that Arabs should not serve.

The fact that 31 and 26 percent of the sons and daughters, independent of their parents' responses, refused to say which political party they supported leads us to surmise that more of them may be inclined to support Rakah than could be assumed by looking only at the distribution of responses of those who indicated the party of their choice. But this is only a guess. In their actual responses, less than 10 percent of the male and female dyads, and of the sons and daughters separately, said they have voted or would vote for Rakah.

Like the female dyads, both the fathers and the sons expected the sons to select their own brides, to be less observant of religious practices, to have interests different than those of the fathers, and to have smaller families.

In final summary, if a social survey was to be conducted twenty years hence among Arabs living in Haifa, Ramla, and Lod, we would expect to find that big changes had occurred in significant aspects of their lives such as how many children they had, their standard of living, their patterns of interaction between the generations and the sexes, and their religious observances. In all of these areas we would expect to find the Arabs behaving more like their Jewish neighbors than like their Arab parents.

Unlike the ultra-Orthodox Jews, who show practically no signs of desiring to take on the ways of the larger culture, the big question about the urban Israeli Arabs is the extent to which their interests in the life styles of the larger Jewish society will be accepted or rejected by the gatekeepers and members of that society. The Israelis' responses probably cannot help but be influenced by the stance that the neighboring Arab countries assume toward them. Should the next twenty years produce peace, or at least an absence of war, and should normal relations develop between Israel and Egypt, Jordan, and/or Syria, then the likelihood of the Arab minority being accepted into the mainstream of Israeli society would be greatly enhanced.

But should the next ten or twenty years produce no significant changes in Arab-Israeli relations, or if tension increases between the Arab states and Israel, then the position of the Arab minority in Israel is likely to worsen and conflict between Jews and Arabs is likely to increase. Acceptance of Israeli Arabs into positions of prestige and influence is likely to decline, and suspicion and a desire to maintain social distance on the part of Jewish Israelis are likely to increase. The responses of the Israeli Arabs to such policies are likely to be bitterness and disappointment, and those feelings are more likely to manifest themselves in more aggressive behavior than has been the case in the past. Ten or twenty years hence a larger proportion of Israeli Arabs, especially those who live in the urban areas, will have availed themselves of the educational opportunities that will allow them to complete secondary school and enter the university where they will be trained to work as lawyers, doctors, executives, engineers, and so on. The refusal of Israeli society to grant them jobs and social positions appropriate to that training and skill will result in much more turmoil than has occurred thus far among the still relatively small group of educated Israeli Arabs.

This survey thus ends on an ironic note. The ultra-Orthodox community faces no obstacles vis-à-vis entry into the larger society. But it shows no interest in doing so and is disdainful and contemptuous of that society. The Israeli Arabs, at least those who live in the cities, are interested in and are moving toward more extensive contacts with and adoption of the practices and life style of the larger society. They, however, in the short run, are likely to find barriers at some of the major entry points to that society. Fearfully, that short run might extend into the next generation.

Notes

Introduction

1 We do not claim that the Arabs and ultra-Orthodox Jews are the *only* such communities in Israel: The Druze and the Circassians are examples of other communities. But we do claim that the two communities we have chosen for study are most important in terms of the consequences that their behavior may have for Israeli society as a whole.

2 The issue of large-scale Russian immigration and the ideological differences that may emerge between these immigrants and Israelis who have been socialized in a democratic-socialist society may also be a serious source of conflict and division.

3 Jerusalem was not included because Arabs and Jews did not live in the same city until Jerusalem was reunited after June 1967.

1. The Jewish ultra-Orthodox and the urban Arab communities: theoretical and geographical comparisons

1 Shortly after the 1967 war when the Israelis were feeling especially proud of themselves and the Arabs were feeling especially humiliated, over 90 percent of the Jewish Israelis answered yes to a question on a public-opinion poll that asked: Would it be better if there were fewer Arabs in Israel? (Bastuni, 1973:417).

2 By acculturation we mean the adoption by a person or group of the culture of another social group.

3 Solomon Poll, *The Hasidic Community of Williamsburg* (New York: Schoken Books, 1969), and Israel Rubin, *Satmar* (Chicago: Quadrangle Books, 1972).

2. Social characteristics and research design

1 This figure does not include the Arab population on the West Bank and Gaza.

2 The census reports that of the foreign born living in Mea Shearim in 1969, 79 percent came from Eastern Europe and 21 percent came from other parts of Europe and the United States.

3 A more detailed discussion of the educational institutions in Mea Shearim appears in Chapter 3.

4 The respondents in the Jewish sample were chosen on the basis of their distinctiveness from the rest of Jewish Israeli society. The urban Arab sample, however, was intended to be representative of the community; and it is to the urban Israeli Arab population as a whole that we expect our findings to generalize.

5 This figure does not include the inhabitants of the territories occupied as a result of the Six Day War in June 1967. (See *Statistical Abstract of Israel,* 1970, Table B/9.)

6 Since the establishment of the state in 1948, Arabs who have lived in the cities have lived in those cities and not in others, such as, for example, Jerusalem or Beersheba. Before 1948 Arabs did live in other cities in Palestine.

7 Indeed, the author tried initially to employ graduate students in the social sciences who have had considerable experience as interviewers, and also contacted various private public-opinion firms in the hope of being able to recruit a field staff. Several of them, however, attempted to obtain interviews and were unable to gain entry into the home or found themselves summarily dismissed because the father had come home, a neighbor entered, and the family was embarrassed at having been found talking to a stranger, or the respondent took offense at a particular question.

8 In about one out of seven times a woman was unwilling to grant an interview until she had asked her husband's permission. About half the time, the husband then refused to have his wife and daughter interviewed.

9 On two occasions, a daughter agreed to be interviewed before her mother's permission was obtained, because the mother was not at home. In both of those instances, when the mother returned, she terminated the interview.

10 The women hardly ever asked the interviewers or me about our religious observances. They were more curious about other aspects of our lives: whether we were married, how we would go about finding a husband, and whether we had children.

11 The Orthodox Jewish male is expected to have his head covered at all times out of respect to God.

12 Some of the mothers claimed that they were "too ignorant" to be able to answer the questions, that it was their husband who ought to be contacted; but in the end they agreed to the interview. There were no instances in which daughters refused.

3. Selective institutions in the two communities

1 In 1965, David Ben Gurion, the former prime minister, withdrew his support from Mapai and organized Rafi. In subsequent elections, however, Rafi has joined the labor coalition.

2 The original "Night of Crystals" occurred in Berlin in 1936. It was a night in which Nazi SA supporters burned and looted synagogues.

3 An official in the Agudat Party observed that most of the voters who live in Mea Shearim go to the voting stations shortly before closing time, which in Israel is almost midnight. They do this, he said, in the hopes that they will not be found out by their Naturei Karta neighbors.

4 At the time of the election for the First Knesset, the Arabs may have been in a state of political shock. Their expectations of a military victory by the Arab states and of the subsequent establishment of an independent Palestinian state had only recently been shattered; the realization that their status had changed from that of a majority one, under the British, to a minority one, under the Jews, was just beginning to be felt.

5 The Mapam Party accepted Arab members after 1954.

6 The other independent school for girls in Mea Shearim is "Beit Yakov, the Old." Before 1948 it was the leading girls' school for the ultra-Orthodox community. But because of its location in Jerusalem, it fell under attack by Jordanian forces during the 1948 war and had to be closed. Following the establishment of the state, some members of the ultra-Orthodox community opted to build a new school rather than undertake the extensive repairs that would be involved in order to restore Beit Yakov to its former condition. But after making some repairs on the building, the school was reopened in the mid-1950s. In 1970, Beit

Yakov had about one-third of the enrollment of B'nat Jerusalem. It accepts children from two years of age into the nursery school; it has an elementary school for first through eighth grades that is in session in the mornings. In the afternoons, there are special classes for girls in their ninth and tenth years of school; but those girls spend most of their time sewing, knitting, and doing other handicrafts activities. They spend a few hours a week on religious subjects. One of the significant differences in the curriculums of B'nat Jerusalem and Beit Yakov is that in the latter Hebrew is taught from the fifth grade. It is taught for three hours a week as a second or foreign language. The main language is Yiddish.

7 The Poalei Agudat Israel Party, whose membership is about half that of Agudat, also publishes a daily newspaper, *Shearim.*

4. A profile of the ultra-Orthodox community in Mea Shearim

1 The 24 percent who are not employed are "students" who have devoted all of their adult lives to the study of the Torah and the Talmud. They spend their days in the yeshiva.

2 At the time of the survey one Israel pound (I.L.) equaled $0.28 in American money. According to the *Statistical Abstract of Israel* (1971) a family of six or more members (average size 7.7) living in an urban center had a monthly income of 947 I.L.

3 According to the *Statistical Abstract of Israel* (1971:163), 78.9 percent of the adult men in Israel watch television regularly (60 percent in their homes) and 95.5 percent listen to the radio every day.

4 According to the *Statistical Abstract of Israel* (1971), 92 percent of the women listen to the radio every day and 73 percent watch television, 60 percent in their own homes.

5 According to the *Statistical Abstract of Israel* (1971), 86 percent of the boys and girls in the fourteen- to seventeen-year-old categories watch television; 64 percent watch it at home.

6 Eighteen years is the legal voting age in Israel.

5. A profile of the urban Arab community in Israel

1 According to the *Statistical Abstract of Israel* (1971), the average monthly income for non-Jews living in urban centers in Israel with an average family size of 6.0 is 601 I.L. As indicated in Chapter 3, the average monthly income for a Jewish family having 6 or more members (average size 7.7) living in an urban center is 947 I.L.

2 As described in Chapter 3, that proportion matches closely the proportion of Arab votes that the Labor Alignment and its predecessor, Mapai, received in past Israeli elections.

3 Readers might wonder whether the respondents were being candid when they answered as they did. Although it is plausible to consider this possibility, their negative reactions to the questions about willingness to have their sons serve in the army and their responses to the voting questions (which match national statistics) are two sensitive topics about which we have reason to believe the responses were candid. These topics are more sensitive than the ones about Israelis' life style.

8. Sex and generational roles in the ultra-Orthodox family

1 Among those not attending there was 76 percent agreement among the dyads as to how many years of schooling the daughters had completed before they stopped and the reasons for their no longer attending school. The disagreement occurred largely because of a "no

answer" by one member of the dyad or a disagreement about whether the daughter had completed eleven or twelve years of school.

9. Sex and generational roles in the urban Arab family

1 Only in response to the question about whether decisions will be made differently in the daughters' homes than in the mothers', did the high proportion of agreement among the dyads (60 percent) signify that most of the daughers and mothers expected similarity between the daughters' life style and their own. Forty-six percent of the dyads said they expected that decisions would be reached jointly between husband and wife in the daughter's household just as it is in the mother's. In total, 80 percent of all the mothers and daughters expected that the daughters would share jointly in the decisions that are made in their households.

References

Anderson, Nels. 1942. *Desert Saints: The Mormon Frontier in Utah.* Chicago: University of Chicago Press.

Avineri, Shlomo. 1973. "Israel: Two Nations?" In Michael Curtis and Mordecai Chertoff, *Israel: Social Structure and Change.* New Brunswick, N.J.: Transaction Books. Pp. 281–306.

Bastuni, Rustum. 1973. "The Arab Israelis." In Michael Curtis and Mordecai Chertoff, *Israel: Social Structure and Change.* New Brunswick, N.J.: Transaction Books. Pp. 409–18.

Bentwich, Joseph Solomon. 1965. *Education in Israel.* London: Routledge and Kegan Paul.

Drummond, William. 1975. "The Jews Who 'Agree' with the PLO." *Los Angeles Times (March 31).*

Eisenstadt, S. N., and Y. Peres. 1965. *Some Problems of Educating a National Minority: A Study of Israeli Education for Arabs.* Washington, D.C.: U.S. Dept. Health, Education, and Welfare.

Gordon, Milton M. 1964. *Assimilation in American Life.* New York: Oxford University Press.

Israeli Central Bureau of Statistics. 1966. *The Settlements of Israel,* vol. 6, no. 28.

Israeli Central Bureau of Statistics. 1970a. *Statistical Abstract of Israel,* no. 21. Jerusalem: Government Press.

1970b. *Results of Elections to the Seventh Knesset and to Local Authorities.* Jerusalem: Government Printing Office.

Jerusalem Post. 1975. "Autopsy Protestors Snatch Body from Shaare Zedek." *Jerusalem Post* (March 2).

Kleinberger, Aharon. 1969. *Society, Schools and Progresses in Israel.* Oxford: Pergamon Press.

Landau, Jacob M. 1969. *The Arabs in Israel: A Political Study.* New York: Oxford University Press.

Layish, Aharon. 1975. "Social and Political Changes in Arab Society in Israel." In Michael Curtis and Mordecai Chertoff, *The Palestinians.* New Brunswick, N.J.: Transaction Books. Pp. 81–8.

Leslie, S. Clement. 1971. *The Rift in Israel: Religious Authority and Secular Democracy.* London: Routledge and Kegan Paul.

Lincoln, C. Eric. 1961. *The Black Muslims in America.* Boston: Beacon Press.

Mansour, Atallah. 1962. "The Modern Encounter Between Jews and Arabs." *New Outlook* 5, no. 3 (March–April).

Marmorstein, Emile. 1969. *Heaven at Bay: The Jewish* Kulturkampf *in the Holy Land.* New York: Oxford University Press.

Poll, Solomon. 1969. *The Hasidic Community of Williamsburg.* New York: Schocken Books.

Rabinowitz, Dorothy. 1972. "Israeli Universities in a Time of Siege." *Change* (February).

Rubin, Israel. 1972. *Satmar: An Island in the City.* Chicago: Quadrangle Books.

Samuel, Edwin. 1969. *The Structure of Society in Israel.* New York: Random House.

Smith, Elmer Lewis. 1958. *The Amish People.* New York: Exposition Press.

Stendel, Ori. 1973. *The Minorities in Israel.* Jerusalem: The Israeli Economist Press.

Weiner, Herbert. 1961. *The Wild Goats of Ein Gedi; A Journal of Religious Encounters in the Holy Land.* Garden City, N.Y.: Doubleday.

Weiss, Charles. 1973. "Government to Help Arab Professionals to Find Suitable Jobs." *Jerusalem Post Weekly.*

Young, Pauline V. 1932. *The Pilgrims of Russian-Town.* Chicago: University of Chicago Press.

Z'uba, Abdul Aziz. 1962. "Education and the Arab Youth." *Outlook* 5, no. 3 (March–April).

Index